MW00655133

The Litigation PR Desk Reference

Richard S. Levick, Esq.
President & CEO
Levick Strategic Communications, LLC
Rlevick@Levick.com

Larry Smith
Director of Strategy
Levick Strategic Communications, LLC
Lsmith@Levick.com

Table of Contents

FOREWORD

No doubt some people, reading the material in this book, may shake their heads and lament, "What a sign of the times! What a disturbing barometer of the world we live in!"

They may be right. *Stop the Presses: The Litigation PR Desk Reference* is a guidebook for attorneys, both in-house and at law firms, and for the companies, organizations and individuals they represent, on how to manage the media during a crisis. It could be an SEC investigation, wholesale thievery by trusted executives, a new product that blows up in consumers' faces or an attack by vocal crusaders. We will talk about how to plan for crises before they occur, how to deal with the media in the critical hours and days as a crisis is first unfolding and what can often be self-interestedly accomplished in the aftermath of a crisis.

Such a text does indeed reflect on our particular world if only because it presupposes a media aggressive enough to air dirty linen on a global basis; enough smoke out there in the corporate ranks to suggest some real fires; and a public hungry for quick news and not always concerned about the supporting facts or lack thereof. It's a noisy world this book reflects on, especially as the echoes of Enron, WorldCom and Tyco will likely reverberate for years to come.

On the other hand, there are lessons here that transcend our specific situation. There has always been corruption. There have always been false accusations. And in most societies mobs have been manipulated to think one thing one moment and something else the next. Remember how pleased the crowd was in Shakespeare's play with Brutus' explanation of why the great Caesar was slain. The very next moment Marc Antony delivers "Friends, Romans, countrymen," and the scales of public opinion tip decisively, fatally, in the opposite direction.

Talk about an effective message point!

Marc Antony's speech was all about art, not science, and so it is important that readers bear a caveat in mind as they read this text. *Stop the Presses* is a guidebook, but not a cookbook. As in any art, the profession of media relations is full of exceptions. Every situation is different, which is why experience is so important. The best practices enumerated here may have to be jettisoned in the heat of battle, and a new, unorthodox, even risky gambit substituted for the tried and true wisdom.

Yet you have to know the rules before you can intelligently break them. At the very least, the rules underscore the fact that crisis planning and crisis management are indeed necessary parts of the arsenal. Even if corporate gods weren't tumbling before our eyes, smart businesses would be thinking about their public liabilities and planning accordingly.

Richard S. Levick, Esq.
Larry Smith

1

What's at Stake?

Here's the quick answer: "Maybe everything."

It is true that the public has a short memory. It is likewise true that yesterday's blaring headlines are tomorrow's footnotes. Bad press is as ephemeral as good press. Unfortunately, the effects of that bad press can be permanent.

Negative press coverage can sabotage stock values. It can torpedo litigation strategies. People may forget the actual scandal or setback that led to a corporate, institutional or personal crisis. But that's cold comfort if it costs you customers you may never recover, or gets you beaten in a lawsuit.

Indeed, litigation offers the most convincing examples of what's at stake, simply because media coverage may directly affect the outcome, even under the best of circumstances. Assume we can effectively isolate a jury from all contact with the media. Assume the judge is above being influenced by anything he or she reads in the newspaper. Even with those advantages, why lead with your chin? If there is not a likelihood of press coverage, generating press coverage might be the dumbest thing you can do. William Sampson, as of this writing the incoming president of DRI (Defense Research Institute, the largest organization of, and resource for, defense firms), recalls a "good Kansas lawyer" who avoided talking with the press because "he knew his judge would rather hear the story first from him than from the newspaper."

Even without press coverage, there may still be a climate of opinion swirling around the case that affects the actions and decisions on both sides. Especially when the stakes are high, hidden agendas are often at play, and those agendas are usually driven—not only by what happens in court—but by how the public perceives the issues. Those perceptions can determine if a case even gets to court. Let's take a look at two very direct, and very different, examples of how media management decisively affected high-stakes litigation. As different as these cases are, they both show what invariably happens when parties to a dispute appreciate the impact of media and the importance of managing media—and what invariably happens when they don't.

The Real Agenda

Media management related to litigation is never more important than in situations where the actual goal of the litigation is—not just to win a case—but to influence the media itself in order to force public opinion in one direction or another. The purpose of some lawsuits is to inspire new legislation. Some litigants file suits to dramatize inequities. Class actions are often all about social policy, not points of law.

Under such circumstances, it behooves the other side to grasp what the hidden agenda really is. A comprehensive case strategy in these cases includes, perforce, media relations. The lawyers must work with other professionals because the client's welfare demands so much else besides legal expertise.

In the post-9/11 environment, a 1996 imbroglio speaks volumes.

One day that year, a hotel franchiser with six hotels under his wing was shocked to learn that he was being sued for discriminating against a Muslim. He was caught totally off guard, with no media team, no media plan and absolutely nothing to say in his defense. Meanwhile, the news cycles, in print and on television, were spinning dizzily. It was a hot story because it was unusual, and because the hotel chain is a brand-name outfit that would attract and keep audience interest.

An outside media team was hired, almost in desperation. (See Chapter 2 for a discussion of media teams, and why they're essential.) Because the story had progressed so far, the PR advisors had to work through the night to get up to speed, devising responses to the allegations and crafting an overriding media strategy. Such a strategy would have to somehow trump the negative messages appearing in editorials and on TV over a seemingly interminable five-day period.

The media team took a good look at the plaintiff's attorney. They read between the lines of his public utterances and scrutinized the kind of media opportunities he was pursuing. It was soon pretty clear that this lawyer had bigger fish to fry than simply negotiating a settlement or even winning a verdict.

In fact, he saw the case as the Islamic equivalent of *Brown v. Board of Education*, as it would spotlight the often uncertain place of Muslims and Muslim-Americans in American society.

The media plan would thus have to address that larger agenda. Without such a plan, even the most effective and direct responses to the specific allegations would fall short of what had to be the real goal, which was to prevent the hotels from becoming a symbol of a larger social inequity.

The plan that was evolved amid the media maelstrom called for an outreach to the Islamic community that would have nothing directly to do with the allegations against the hotel—as was appropriate, since the allegations themselves were not the real stake in the matter.

The solution was for the hotel's legal counsel to call a leading Islamic-American public interest group and offer a wide range of services to the Islamic community. The public interest group was delighted with the offer and disengaged from the hotel chain controversy. It was convinced that the defendant was sincere in his demonstration of good will. There would be no public castigation of the hotel franchiser or the chain, not from this key interest group.

Instant media training of the hotel franchiser, heretofore a reluctant and shy spokesperson, followed by television appearances with a heartfelt *mea culpa*, made the story disappear within 24 hours.

What to Do, What Not to Do

Simpler cases mandate simpler media-relations lessons. One potentially devastating libel case offers a fundamental example of common sense in media relations. It is a compelling reminder to respect the media, and to bear in mind how badly the media can hurt you if you do not respect it.

In 1997, a plaintiff's attorney in Little Rock named

Sandy McMath contacted a small-circulation newsletter, *Inside Litigation*, with a case that no one else was covering, at least not at that point. It was a libel suit against the publishing companies Grove/Atlantic, Inc. and Penguin Books USA Inc., and it was a hot enough story for the editor at *Inside Litigation* to jump all over.

It concerned *Land of Opportunity*, a book that covered the careers of four brothers and how they grew up to become notorious drug dealers. The book depicted their mother, Hazel Chambers, as a prostitute, although there was no evidence whatsoever to support that characterization.

McMath patiently explained the details of his case to the *Inside Litigation* reporter without being inflammatory or tendentious. In contrast, the defense attorney, a partner at a global law firm, refused all comment, which meant that the coverage was going to be totally slanted toward the plaintiff's side.

But that wasn't the worst of it. The defense spokesperson was, by turn, dismissive, obdurate and self-entitled. He was aghast that the publication was even bothering to cover the case.

When the reporter informed her editor of the defense attorney's bumptious response, she was told to just write what she had, and that he would take a few extra steps of his own. Sensing an opportunity to promote his publication in a national outlet, he sent all the details of the case to *The New York Times*, which expressed keen interest in an email reply. (*Inside Litigation* published a long feature on the Chambers case in its October 1997 edition.)

As the editor now reflects, he would have been less reactive had the defense attorney given some reasonable explanation for his continuing "no comments" to such questions as "Did you check police records to confirm any evidence of prostitution?" and "Is there a movie deal in the works?" In fact, the editor might never have thought to call *The Times*, despite the promotional value, but for the defense attorney's persistent incivility.

The Times never did run the story, but McMath was informed of its interest and he naturally saw no reason to hide it from the opposition. The case may have been weakening on its merits, but the threat of national exposure

What's at Stake: The Loyalty of Major Clients

Law firms make a decisive mistake when they ignore or glibly underestimate the demand by major clients that they develop and aggressively apply media relations and crisis management skills.

Consider DaimlerChrysler. This global giant insists, not requests, that outside counsel demonstrate just such skills as a crucial component of case strategy.

"We expect our lawyers to understand some fundamental business principles, not the least of which is that the damage to a company's reputation after a case is over can far exceed, in actual dollars, the costs of the lawsuit itself," says Steven Hantler, assistant general counsel for government and regulation.

In fact, in the late 1990s, DaimlerChrysler "institutionalized" proactive media relations after the company was caught short in the press following an adverse judgment. According to Hantler, the corporation "directly and formally" advised its law firms that they would need to participate on the media end of their cases as either spokespersons or strategists or both. Some firms were "skeptical, even resistant," says Hantler. Others, like Gibson, Dunn & Crutcher, enthusiastically rose to the occasion and have continued to support the client's commitment to communicate its side of every story.

"We realized that plaintiffs' attorneys were aggressively draw- ing first blood in the media, and that their attacks often went unanswered," says Hantler. "We simply made it unacceptable, in many cases, for any of our lawyers to respond to those attacks with a 'no comment.' We were no longer interested in ceding the [media] field to our opponents."

Hantler believes that, with most corporate litigation, the press prefers to talk to in-house counsel. But there is certainly a role for DaimlerChrysler's outside lawyers to comment on the record as well. The company expects that commentary to be in plain English and devoid of legalese, to arrive in 30-second sound bites and to demonstrate the lawyers' real passion for the cause at hand.

At the very least, law firms must participate in all relevant media strategy sessions at DaimlerChrysler "to help us project the trajectory of case-related issues and how those issues will likely play out in the press in the months or years ahead," says Hantler.

Ideally, outside counsel will so warm to the task that they will adapt the beneficial effects to their trial strategies. DaimlerChrysler wants lawyers who instinctively understand that the message points they need to develop will have the same impact in court as in the media.

After all, the audience is really the same in both instances.

was one important factor persuading the defense to settle faster and, presumably, for more money.

Certainly, the defense is often constrained from commenting on a case, and the plaintiffs have a natural advantage in the media as a result. But, as the sidebar explains, there are ways to level the playing field or, at least, minimize the disadvantage.

McMath was able to win the media skirmish in the Chambers case because—no less than the media advisors counseling the beleaguered hotel franchiser in our previous example—he had an instinctive sense for what was at stake.

That sense extends beyond any single lawsuit. "When you comment in the press, or publish an article in a respected journal, you become part of an ongoing professional dialogue," he says. "You become an opinion-maker. For example, I have published articles on tobacco liability and insurance funds in journals that I knew judges read.

"You must also get the ear of your colleagues on both sides," adds McMath, who has pioneered cases once thought impossible to win, given the media's sturdy First Amendment protection. With a track record of suing newspapers and publishers, McMath has been acutely conscious of just how important it is to maintain friendly relations with the newspapers and publishers he isn't suing.

By appreciating the role of the media, you gain a subtle public imprimatur for your position that is persuasive to friend and foe alike. "What seems like a frivolous case becomes something else entirely when other attorneys see it discussed as a serious substantive matter in a responsible publication," says McMath. Suddenly, summary judgment doesn't seem quite so reliable. On the contrary, a protracted and well-planned media outreach can bring defendants to the settlement table right at the get-go.

Early Warning Signs

The hotel owner in our case study above was utterly blindsided by a crisis that he didn't stand much chance of anticipating and planning for. At the same time, crisis managers can take a longer view, foreseeing crises well in advance, if they are instinctively sensitive to the macro-economic and political factors that are breeding grounds for media inquisitions. For example:

What is the industry environment?

Other cases of a crisis nature in your industry are being covered in the media. A reporter in an industry trade publication has started to ask about facts related to what now looks to be a "trend story." Certain industries are more vulnerable to trend stories. Is the industry bleeding, like telecom? The perception is that, as profits go south, everyone is a suspect because everyone is desperate. Is the

What's At Stake: Lessons from a Libel Case

Plaintiffs' attorney Sandy McMath had a game plan: Get the word out on the libel case he was litigating, get it out now, and get it out responsibly. The defense side had no media plan whatsoever, nor any willingness to even play the game. The defense attorney high-handed an obscure newsletter and his client suffered.

The defense case was probably too weak to take to court, although First Amendment defenses can be hard to break. In any event, if you do have to settle a case, effective media planning can at least give you a stronger position at the negotiating table. The advantage always goes to the side that millions of media consumers have been persuaded to support. In its very simplicity, McMath's case offers powerful lessons about the power of the media, and how to survive it:

- No publication is too small not to take seriously. True, if there is a deluge of media requests during a major crisis, you will need to prioritize the publications on your call-back list. But, especially in a day and age when advanced technology can track so much information, any article in any publication can affect your litigation strategy as well as your company's reputation.

- Reasonably explain why you cannot speak on the record. Doing so might suggest that, if you could talk, you'd say something persuasive. In McMath's case, the journalist had no reason to assume the defense side had anything exculpatory to offer even if the lawyer were empowered to offer it.

- Because you have explained why you can't go public, there's now some trust on the part of the reporter. At that point, go off the record and suggest pointed questions that the reporter might ask the other side. If you can't litigate in the press overtly, you may be able to do so covertly.

- Establish human contact with reporters. Use their first names when you talk to them. Always be polite! Remember Mark Twain's famous warning: Don't pick fights with people who buy ink by the barrel.

industry such a repository of public trust that one betrayal of that trust—by, say, Arthur Andersen—guarantees media interest in other global accounting firms?

Regulatory environment

The Department of Justice or the Securities and Exchange Commission or a member of Congress has indicated they want to watch a particular issue more closely, or political pressure is building to find a whipping boy. Every time Elliot Spitzer sneezes, the media says, "Gesundheit!" Watch every signal his office sends. Likewise, monitor state attorneys general in all states where your client or firm has a major presence. State AGs are political animals, and your back may be a good stepladder to power.

> *"What seems like a frivolous case becomes something else entirely when other attorneys see it discussed as a serious substantive matter in a responsible publication," advises Sandy McMath, who has pioneered cases against the media once thought impossible to win.*

Stock performance

For two consecutive quarters, the corporate numbers are down. Coverage of the stock decline is painful enough, but reporters will jump at any suggestion that shareholder pressures are forcing inappropriate or illegal responses. At the very least, they will be inspired by the down numbers to sniff around for other negatives. Since you need to prepare a media response that includes positive messages about the stock declines, include as part of that preparation some discussion of what those other negatives might be, and how you should respond.

Bad performance news is always reason for any company to go on full media alert.

Stockholder actions

Any action by shareholders legitimizes media interest in every aspect of the company's life. Remember too, lawsuits that name directors and officers often lead to personal interest in the directors and officers themselves. You must anticipate full background checks by reporters. Read the resumes of your directors and officers very carefully. Were any of them ever short sellers? Were any of them ever sued before? How did they get their current jobs, and why? Prepare to defend them as if they were suspects in a crime.

Dangerous practices

Enron got into a lot of trouble with off-balance-sheet assets. Crooked financiers in the 1980s were associated with junk bonds. In fact, off-balance-sheet assets and junk bonds are both perfectly legitimate. But if Enron misuses its instruments, or Boesky his, you can expect to be called by a suspicious reporter and asked to explain what you're up to if you use them.

Hostile takeovers

As we learned in the 1980s, hostile takeovers open vast frontiers of self-interest. There are a zillion reasons for all sorts of people on both sides of the takeover to say all sorts of things to the media. During a hostile situation, you need to monitor every syllable that gets uttered in public and anticipate those that are about to be uttered.

Non-governmental organizations

You don't need to be the target of a nonprofit organization to go on full alert. Simply be in the industry—as a NAFTA trade partner or an international lender—and you may become the next target. (For more on NGOs, see Chapter 11.) Monitor the NGO Web sites and press appearances and think differently about the media if they are targeting the firm or industry next door.

Hot-button issues

Could the obesity cases have been foreseen? Perhaps not, but listen closely for public rumblings that might suggest incipient adversarial interest in your product. For example, many people don't like SUVs. They don't like them for policy reasons ("they guzzle gas"), and they don't like them for political reasons ("people who drive them are suburbanites who don't see the world like us urban animals"). There has already been ample suggestion that SUVs aren't safe either—and we all know where those kinds of suggestions lead.

Past escapes

The Catholic Church incited keen media interest a decade ago with sexual misconduct charges that soon departed the front page after a leading church official was exonerated. But what could possibly have led to the conclusion that the issue would not someday resurface? Corporations, with less painful liabilities should never relax after a brush with scandal or fail to prepare for the media's unwanted return to an unpleasant subject.

Qui tam

What internal dynamics might lead to a public crisis? Have there been widespread layoffs? Is the company known for tough, unreasonable managers? Does employee dissatisfaction hang palpably like a shroud in the home office? Such an environment can foster whistleblowers who will talk to the press, as well as to the government, just a little more readily and a little more enthusiastically, than in a less strained culture.

Faulty products

Pintos do explode. Asbestos does kill. Any genuine product liability matter that crosses the desk of in-house counsel should be treated, for media purposes, as if lawsuits have already been filed and reporter inquiries phoned in. The problem may go away quietly with a responsible corporate initiative. But don't assume it will, and prepare as if it won't.

Not all crises arise or can necessarily be detected from scenarios similar to the above. In fact, some crises come from nowhere. They often involve a hostile reporter who's picked up on something that, from your perspective, is breathtakingly trivial. A permanent media team can hypothesize possible exposures—when, for example, a reporter who was hostile to you when he was writing for a local newspaper suddenly gets a job with a national daily.

Remember, media professionals are trained to track not only the news, but the people who report it.

In the next two chapters, we will discuss how to put a media team—armed with an effective media plan—in place sooner rather than later, preferably before a problem arises.

So Don't Forget...

A few fundamental facts underscore just how much is usually at stake when the press trains its focus on your lawsuit...

- The lawsuit itself may be just a small part of what you're up against. First, you must determine what larger agendas drive the litigation. Victory in the press may actually be more important than victory in court.

- Take all publications seriously. A misstep with the editor of a 200-subscriber newsletter can affect coverage in *The New York Times*. Today's information technology is too comprehensive. Don't be cavalier with any reporter.

- Even a minor lawsuit takes on serious dimension if, for whatever reason, a reporter decides to cover it. Suddenly, the garden-variety commercial dispute ostensibly dramatizes an important trend in an industry. Suddenly, the obscure wrongful discharge case ostensibly confirms a long-established pattern of racism.

- Major clients no longer ask that their attorneys be media-savvy, they demand it! As far as they're concerned, the risk to their corporate reputation after litigation is often much greater, in sheer dollars and cents, than the costs and penalties of the lawsuit itself.

2

The Quintessential Crisis Team: Two Approaches

O ne fact is inescapable: Any organization that is likely to find itself on trial in the court of public opinion must have a crisis team in place that includes people able to put a response plan in motion immediately when a crisis arrives.

Most of the major players in high-risk industries have long understood the need for effective crisis teams. For the automobile manufacturers, airlines, big pharma, alcohol and, certainly, the tobacco industry, crisis is a fact of life and a cost of doing business. Tires blow, planes crash, pills have side effects, drunks drive and governments sue. Without a systemic organizational structure in place, these companies would simply not be grappling with the reality of their businesses.

What the crisis team consists of and how it is structured will vary from company to company. Multinational health care corporations are different from banks, banks are different from accounting firms, accounting firms are different from regional construction companies, and so forth.

Within each category, there are also salient differences among organizations. The organization chart at one airline might not look at all like the organization chart at a competitor airline. Some are centralized, and some are decentralized. Reporting relationships might vary from one corporation to another as a result.

Organizational Fit

In setting forth crisis team prescriptions, the first variable to consider is size. Some tobacco giants have deemed it necessary to have large permanent teams in place. But it is impossible for many smaller companies to assume the fixed overhead of an internal team. Even companies with $100 million or more in revenue might be hard pressed to justify such an investment.

However, smaller companies are still not exempt from

having to have adequate human resources available. One obvious option is to rely on an outside team at a public relations agency. In some cases, that will entail a monthly retainer or other fee arrangement less onerous than the cost of permanent employees.

Alternatively, smaller companies and organizations can work out arrangements whereby the outside agency creates a crisis team ready to swing into action if called upon to do so. They might bill hourly fees to set up the team and periodically review the company's crisis plan, or to digest new information or developments that will be relevant should a crisis occur.

Among corporations, the crisis teams may need to mirror the organization chart. If a company is decentralized, with numerous and relatively independent business units around the world, those units might need crisis team members knowledgeable on local issues and the local corporate culture. Sometimes, a team member in New York can adequately master the fact pattern surrounding a crisis in Frankfurt. Other times, that crisis may require language capabilities, knowledge of local law, personal relations with local media and a sense for local public opinion that only someone closer to the situation can provide.

At the same time, some major crises require company-wide coordination of effort. No matter how decentralized the organization, it is therefore essential that, in the event of such a crisis, a plan be in effect to bring all the disparate crisis team members into one unified whole, with clearly defined roles and lines of authority.

Another important variable is the law department, since all crisis teams need to include legal counsel. In forming crisis teams, it is necessary to confer with the chief legal officer as to which lawyers will be included. Again, some law departments are highly decentralized. Here too, local lawyers might need to be members of local teams but adapt to a company-wide team at a moment's notice.

The structures of some law departments, like General Electric's, are flat. Individual attorneys function almost like partners at a law firm, with their own specific expertise. In these cases, the team formation is easier, as a single lawyer with public affairs experience can be the crisis team's point person.

Two examples of global crisis teams clearly demonstrate how different organizational structures dictate different approaches. Yet in both instances, a similar fundamental objective is achieved: the ready deployment of media-savvy experts able to maximize information flow, handle multiple tasks during a crisis, and deliver a coherent and credible message to the public.

In both cases, the formation of a team and the creation of a crisis plan (see Chapter 3 for more on crisis plans) occur before an actual crisis. Nothing is more essential than to be proactive and set up the structure ahead of time. Once a crisis occurs, there won't likely be time to start interviewing candidates for the job.

Brand-based Paradigm

At Michelin North America, Nancy Banks, director, public relations, supervises a team of two media professionals, with a third person available during a crisis. But a pool of about 50 executives and specialists at various points in the corporation can be immediately added to the team as needed.

Some of these team members are in-house lawyers or C-suite executives. Others are division heads. Others are technical specialists. These are the "content experts" who provide the crucial information that the media and the public require in crisis situations.

As a 14-year Michelin veteran, Banks knows these 50 people personally and can pick all the adjuncts required for the team as soon as a crisis breaks. Team members can access a proprietary Web site in the event of a crisis. All potential team members are profiled on the Web site. If Banks were out of commission, the team formation could thus still go forward. No one would have to worry about identifying the in-house experts or scurry around looking for contact information while the crisis was breaking.

While the Web site and expert pool guarantee that the right people are assigned to a crisis, the team strategy at Michelin is also determined by which of the several Michelin brands is affected. Banks oversees the Michelin brand in the replacement market and the overall corporate reputation. But the responsibilities of the two media specialists who report to her are further divided among two other brands: Uniroyal and B.F. Goodrich, as well as the various business units, such as truck tires, cycle tires, etc. "Original equipment" (i.e., the unit that supplies products to vehicle manufacturers) is also treated as a separate division.

Again, organizational structure affects crisis team strategy. A Michelin brand issue might involve corporate and legal as well as product issues. Uniroyal and Goodrich brand issues are usually consumer-oriented. The "original equipment" unit is business-to-business, with some direct consumer impact as well. Michelin's strategy assigns responsibility for each to different team members.

Michelin uses an outside PR agency as part of the total crisis team. During a crisis, outside feedback from the agency is often useful as part of the planning process. However, Banks believes that the spokespersons must be from the company itself. It's a matter of credibility, of showing the world that you take the situation seriously enough to handle it yourself.

Once the team is assembled, decisions are made on such crucial questions as, "Do we take a proactive approach and call the media, or do we wait for them to call us?" According to Banks, the answer is always guided by: "What would our customers want us to do?" This is good public relations, not just a platitude. For consumer-oriented companies like Michelin, consumers are the final tribunal in any controversy.

Crisis management is a democratic process made possible, says Banks, by a corporate culture that enjoys a significant element of "mutual trust." Early in any crisis, Banks will ask, "Is there anything here we need to be ashamed of?" In this particular corporate culture, she feels she'll get an honest answer.

The decision-making is efficient, albeit democratic, because the team members have been shrewdly selected for their individual expertise. Banks will not question the input of a quality manager who has specific product expertise, nor would that manager likely question Banks' assessment of how a particular statement will be greeted by the media.

At the same time, debate between the media experts

and legal team members is "healthy." There will always be conflicts between PR professionals and lawyers. The PR instinct is to disclose; the legal instinct is to protect, or to at least be more guarded. Some PR strategies may convince a skeptical public but open the door to a blizzard of litigation, however groundless and unfair it might be. Some legal strategies will exonerate the company in court but alienate the buying public.

Only by allowing for open and sometimes heated debate can the best middle course be determined. In one instance, the legal concerns may be overruled if widespread litigation is finally determined to be an acceptable cost of doing business, and that the highest priority is to convince the world that you are right and ready to prove it in court. Alternatively, the PR concerns may be overruled if there are legal points so important that a protracted public silence is the better part of valor.

Ironic Paradigm

If Michelin is a global company that requires different team strategies for different brands, Arthur Andersen was a global organization actuated by a very different concern. With all such professional services firms, the driving need, in or out of crisis, is to confirm a singular global integrity. Generally speaking, at global partnerships (and especially law firms), a partner in Chicago is jointly and severally liable for the behavior of a partner in Caracas. Andersen, with separate partnerships set up in different countries, was something of an exception to that rule. But with Andersen too, clients will still want to be sure that a common ethic ensures consistency everywhere.

Interestingly, we know of no better model for how to set up and manage a crisis team than Andersen's. It is indeed an irony that a firm that endured one of the worst media blitzes in modern history should be such a paradigm, especially as the media campaign implemented by the team ultimately failed to save the day.

Andersen's demise does not belie the soundness of Andersen's media planning or the seaworthiness of its team. The Andersen experience offers a profound caveat to all essays on crisis planning, including our own.

The dismal lesson is that some crises are terminal, either because the company is guilty of unforgivable transgressions, or because there are times when no one will believe anything you say, no matter how well directed the media response. It is essential to remember that Andersen's team, set up before the Enron debacle, had always been effective in its handling of media relations for a variety of lawsuits and other institutional skirmishes.

The Andersen crisis-team strategy typifies planning for large partnerships that, however diverse, must fasten on consistent firm-wide messages.

First, set up a crisis committee. This is your central planning group, as well as the entity from which all other team components can be spun. At organizations like Andersen, the committee typically includes:

- A decision-maker, either the CEO or a senior player reporting to the CEO. This individual must be able to make a determination on all actions and responses at every stage of a crisis, without having to clear it with anyone

- Two or three experienced PR professionals and lobbyists

- Two or three lawyers.

The immediate purpose of the crisis committee is to articulate the organization's business goals as a guide to all subsequent crisis strategy. Are we trying to save a particular client base? Are we trying to prove that a particular product or service is unaffected by an ongoing crisis? Are we trying to influence the media in a particular geographic region because we plan to open a new office there?

Second, as Chris Hinze, former worldwide director of communications for Andersen Legal, puts it, the crisis committee's function is to "cascade" policy to subteams in other affected regions, countries and cities. Thus, at Andersen, the crisis committee was nationally based in the firm's Chicago headquarters and its Washington, D.C., office. It included staff with expertise in PR, legal and lobbying. In turn, smaller Andersen teams in London and Hong Kong communicated 24/7 with the worldwide team and with countries in their own time zones to ensure the most consistent message delivery possible.

Third, get your outside media advisors in place and define their roles. At Andersen, outside PR firms were used around the world for three main purposes: to provide independent third-party feedback, to help craft message points, and to deal with the flood of incoming media calls. (For more on crafting message points, see Chapter 4.) As at Michelin, the overall policy and day-to-day media contacts were handled by the in-house team.

The Right Stuff

Such formidable responsibility raises the question: What qualifications should companies look for when staffing crisis teams?

As Hinze observes, the team members must naturally be "calm and objective," and they have to like this kind of work. Some PR professionals are great publicists, but they're accustomed to living on the sunny side of the street. They often succeed in getting their companies' business successes noticed, and they know how to get stories published. But they don't necessarily know how to prevent stories from getting published, nor do they recognize that they're in a life-threatening fight where you have to live with bad coverage and still battle to get your messages out.

It's relatively easy to hire battle-tested communications people. You simply ask them if they've ever been involved in a media brouhaha. If so, you call their former bosses and ask how they handled themselves.

Of the two professionals who report to Banks, one was hired because of PR-agency experience, and the other because of a solid background in community affairs. "Crisis management was not really a consideration when they were hired," says Banks, in part because Michelin has never undergone an ordeal as devastating as the Firestone fracas, much less the Andersen collapse.

In any event, it may not be advisable or practicable to segregate your crisis talent and your promotional or business-to-business staff. Ideally, you want team members capable of handling both sides of the media. "When a major crisis hits, your whole communications staff has to shift into crisis mode and simply forget about doing anything else for the duration," says Hinze.

It's simply less efficient when some business-to-business publicists are able to make the shift, while others still try to conduct business as usual—especially since every journalist in the country just wants to talk about the crisis. Moreover, a talent for handling crisis only makes for better B-to-B. Publicists with a fine-tuned instinct for apprehending problems are able to think faster on their feet, whatever they're selling.

Disparate Examples, Common Lessons

Michelin North America and Andersen show how different organizational structures require different approaches to setting up and managing a crisis team. Michelin is a brand-oriented manufacturer with crisis team members assigned to individual brands. Andersen was a global professional service charged with the delivery of consistent firm-wide messages.

Michelin has never been subjected to withering global scrutiny for alleged malfeasance. Andersen most certainly was.

Because they're so different, the common lessons suggested by the experiences of both organizations are all the more significant. These are the fundamental best practices that apply universally in crisis situations, relevant to all types of corporate or professional team formation. For example:

- The crisis team must be in place, with responsibilities clearly delineated, before a crisis occurs.

- An outside PR agency is a good sounding board for ideas and strategies. But the communications themselves—the actual work of media management during a crisis—must come from the organization's own people. An agency can supply additional arms and legs but ownership of the problem cannot be delegated.

- Technology is always an essential tool. Andersen used a Web site so its team could unleash a torrent of information. Michelin uses a Web site to guarantee that the right experts will be assigned to the right crises whenever and wherever they occur.

- It is essential to have lawyers and lobbyists on the crisis team and to encourage open debate among all professional experts. Their instincts are different, and companies must weigh both in the balance in making every important decision during a crisis.

- Arguably, the crisis team should include business-to-business publicists. The skills complement each other. By being close to a particular brand or practice, the publicist can provide valuable information. And gaining crisis skills makes publicists better all-around communicators.

- Crisis team members must enjoy the challenge of a crisis or keep out of the way.

So Don't Forget...

Crisis management is labor-intensive. To manage well, you need a team in place, and you need to apply a number of best practices when you staff that team.

- Set up the team now. Once a crisis occurs, there won't likely be time to start interviewing candidates for the job.

- The team should usually reflect the company's organizational structure. Highly decentralized companies ought to have communications people stationed in different offices. But the overall team structure should allow for efficient decision-making by the team heads, based on input from the far-flung crisis and media managers.

- Include lawyers on the team, and encourage respectful debate between the lawyers and the communications specialists. They bring very different perspectives to the table. Input from both sides is critical if an adequate crisis response is to evolve.

- Pick only team members who enjoy the challenge of this kind of work.

3

The Crisis Plan:
From Action Points to Talking Points

When a crisis arises, the normal response is to either freeze or panic. At corporations, the meltdown can naturally be more spectacular than at smaller companies or with individuals, since many more players are involved. Not knowing what to do, people do nothing, assuming someone else will do it. Even worse, they act, but they act ill-advisedly or at odds with each other.

In such an environment, the media can have a field day. Today, most corporations have crisis plans in place that are activated at the first hint of crisis. A tobacco company or an airline without a crisis plan is unthinkable.

The plan obviously cannot anticipate the specifics of the crisis. But it does provide a framework for going forward coherently. For example, crisis-team formation (discussed in Chapter 2) is inextricably bound up with the crisis plan, simply because the plan usually begins with the necessary steps for assembling the team and assigning responsibilities.

Thus, Michelin's proprietary Web site is the first place people go when there is a crisis, as all potential team members are profiled there. Director, public relations Nancy Banks, or a surrogate if Banks is unavailable, goes directly to the Web site and picks the names she'll need. That is Step One in the Michelin crisis plan.

Rational Reaction

Once a team is assembled in the same room, or via conference call, the media plan provides a template that allows for organized response. Because the crisis plan is created ahead of time, in a calmer environment, it is comprehensive. No vital particulars get lost in the heat of the moment. Thus, questions like, "Should we be proactive with the media or wait for them to call us?" are included as part of the template, guaranteeing that vital point will be covered as early in the crisis as possible.

The plan can list discussion points that dig even deeper. If, for example, the determination is made to be proactive with the media, a follow-up question might be, "Shall we distribute our phone numbers to key press contacts or simply place a few calls?"

At Michelin, the crisis plan itself is posted on the Web site as an organizational tool for everyone with a need to know. A statement is also posted on the site, usually a simple acknowledgement that a situation has arisen and here is our preliminary response. The statement is adjusted as events develop.

The appropriate people are assigned to gather information about what happened and who was affected. Almost any information can turn out to be important further down the line, so it's veritable detective work that's called for at this point. If a tornado has damaged a plant, how was the rest of the community affected? What are other companies experiencing? Following the crisis plan, certain team members will check the effects on inventory—how many tires were destroyed, ancillary damage to the plant, etc.

Following the crisis plan, the media team is brought in at a point where the preliminary information-gathering by the company is already underway and the news of the crisis has circulated. It's at this point that the question of being proactive with the media arises. Preliminary message points are also drawn up. They will be expanded or refined as events unfurl.

The next step in the crisis plan calls for action by Michelin personnel, specifically on two fronts: Who do we need to help? Who do we need to contact?

The tornado example is a pointed one, as a Michelin plant in Fort Wayne, Indiana, was damaged by a severe storm a few years ago. "Who to help" obviously encompasses employees and their families or other members of the community that the company can assist. "Who to contact" would include government officials and possibly other businesses in the community, as well as the media.

Again, as these actions are set in motion in accordance with the plan, the earlier tasks usually need to be revisited. More information will need to be incorporated on the Web

Al Gore Invented It...Why Not Use It?

Companies like Michelin use their Web sites as tools for aggressive message delivery, as well as for crisis management. They complement blast emails, position ads and direct pitching as routes to the press, shareholders, opponents, employees or the general public.

These sites may be deployed as an extension of a main corporate Web site or with their own URL. They are simultaneously messaging and case-management tools. For example, the sites can include substantive case-related statements; background on the company as a "good citizen;" case background (with information on the opposing side, the judge, the court, the hearing history, etc.); updates and press releases.

As a vehicle for broader press relations, the sites can review past cases, including ones that had unfavorable outcomes, creating a context where the company can talk about what it has done to correct the problems that surfaced during those cases.

But there's a guiding rule: if you're going to use the Web, keep it simple for both internal and external users. "Communications extranets and Web sites must be easier to use than amazon.com and extremely fast to deploy," says Justin Szlasa, president, Triplebridge Consulting Ltd.

"Our clients prepare Web sites and extranets ahead of time, ensure their response teams are well trained, and then keep the Web sites and extranets in their holsters," adds Szlasa. "They can have a site up and running within minutes to get any information to anyone."

site, and the message points or the media crisis plan itself might change.

The next item on the crisis plan is: What don't we know at this point that we need to know? And, how do we find it out? If a severe storm hits Fort Wayne, a main question to answer at this point is, "Will the plant be inoperative and for how long?"

By now, we're no longer dealing with a natural disaster or common enemy. Suddenly, there's a PR liability as well, since the community will want to know if people will lose their jobs, or if Michelin even intends to repair or replace the facility. (After the Fort Wayne tornado, repairs were made quickly, no jobs were lost, and there were no injuries to workers.)

The crisis plan thus allows for a neat transition from administrative disaster planning to a potentially more delicate media planning, from action points to talking points.

Fifteen Million House Calls

It's not just high-risk industries such as air transportation or tobacco that are particularly attuned to the need to have a crisis plan in place. Any major retailer should know that in the event of a crisis a massive corporate stonewall will likely alienate customers and jeopardize revenue worldwide.

Corporate Crisis Plans Are Sanity Tools

Crisis plans are templates for corporate survival. They provide a structure for a coherent response so that dozens, maybe hundreds, of unofficial spokespersons won't be running around like Chicken Little or, just as bad in some situations, doing nothing and saying nothing. The crisis plan allows a variety of professionals to gather together at once and systematically cover all the bases, methodically plotting their action points and message points.

Michelin's approach typifies at least five advantages of advance planning, without which no corporate crisis plan is complete:

- It utilizes simple technology—a Web site—to organize the agenda.

- The plan itself allows for the formation of an organized team drawn from the ranks of the entire company.

- It allows for thorough information-gathering.

- It provides a preliminary media response and forces the crisis team to strategize a specific media plan sooner rather than later.

- It forces the crisis team to articulate questions to which they don't yet have answers but will need sooner rather than later.

The very existence of a crisis plan creates an immediate awareness in the corporate ranks that some response is needed or that a decision to not respond at least be conscious and strategic. It's all about "ensuring that management understands that bad news doesn't age well," says Nancy Banks, Michelin's director, public relations.

The ideal crisis plan is one that takes on a life of its own, mobilizing people for responsible action simply because there's a plan in force that calls on them to take that action.

Sears, Roebuck and Co. is a major retailer.

The company knows that bad press of any sort isn't only about reputation. It's about money. In 2002, for instance, Sears had over 25 million active credit customers. Over the years, the company's diversified holdings included real estate development units like Homart (divested in the mid-1990s) as well as financial services.

Sears employees make 15 million house calls to customers every year. Trouble can thus come from anywhere, and the effects of real trouble could be inestimable. That being the case, it's surprising that, as Jan Drummond, Sears' former senior director, external communications, confirms, the company did not have a formal crisis plan in place until 2000.

The reason may reflect one of the important points we made in Chapter 2: Media management requires the enthusiastic and responsive participation of the in-house legal team.

When Sears finally did write a formal crisis plan, the timing coincided with the in-house rise of then general counsel Anastasia Kelly, who by all accounts is an unusually gifted legal manager with a keen eye for how different parts of the corporate picture must fit together. There's a lot more to running a law department than the law.

Drummond believes that the success she's had in both creating and implementing a crisis plan is directly attributable to the fact that any of her team members can consult with any member of the law department at any time. "Sometimes we must get an immediate answer to a question," says Drummond. "Our communications staff members know they can interrupt the lawyers during a meeting or grab them in the hall."

The crisis plan grew out of a series of brown-bag lunches that Drummond held with what would become known as her "Critical Incident Communications" team. They developed a worksheet based on a series of What Ifs—What if the company is involved in a hostile takeover? What if a plane crashes into one of the stores?

Specific follow-ups were posed. How much media coverage would one situation generate versus another? Are there opportunities amid the crisis to get out positive

The 'Crisis Wire':
One Indispensable Piece of the Plan

Communications professionals wisely focus on Web sites as an item on the corporate crisis plan to provide breaking developments for reporters as well as basic information and updates on natural disasters or accidents.

At the same time, crisis plans should also deploy external resources. Commercial newswires allow corporate communicators to target a wide audience, including the mass media, independent journalists, the investment community and the general public—virtually simultaneously—speaking in their own words in the timeliest way possible.

Companies that develop their messages fast enough can enjoy a potentially crucial jump on adversaries or possibly hostile reporters. "It really is the crisis wire," says Dave Armon, president of PRNewswire Americas, which offers a diverse distribution network for targeting mass audiences with breaking news and messages. (Visit prnewswire.com/news for a full sampling.)

PRNewswire's PRN Direct, for example, is a secure extranet that allows members to upload press releases for distribution. (Clients can also email or fax press releases to PRNewswire.) After a short sender-verification process, the press release is distributed to the media and financial community and (as of this writing) to 3,600 Web sites, including the major search engines. While around 60 percent of the *Fortune* 500 uses PRNewswire to distribute press releases, at-risk industries are among the most loyal users. For example, according to Armon, virtually every U.S. airline is a member.

Through PRNewswire, a corporation can announce in the first moments of a crisis when fuller information will be forthcoming and follow up with the press release as soon as it's ready.

In a war of words or during a crisis, the online race is to the swift. If a corporation gets its side of a crisis onto a private newswire fast enough, its statement may be the only source that journalists will have for hours. Even though it's duly identified as an official release, the message dissemination can dramatically level the playing field in the initial struggle for media sympathy. Remember, a lot of reporters identify the good guys and bad guys in the first few minutes of a breaking story.

Another important weapon in the crisis communications arsenal allows members to monitor the vast number of Internet sites for the latest account of the crisis at hand. Services such as eWatch™ from PRNewswire monitor thousands of sites and provide daily reports to the corporate communicators.

Being proactive online is, in any event, a smart practice at every stage in the life of the story. It is, after all, where the people who write the story now live.

messages about the company, and how should those be expressed in the context of a tragedy or a scandal?

The document that evolved from these meetings, called the Critical Incident Communication worksheet, is now the de facto Sears crisis plan. By hypothesizing the media dimensions of certain kinds of crises, and investing considerable time in the process, Drummond and her team began to define audiences—the relatives of victims, civic leaders, customers, shareholders, etc.—and articulate possible responses to a variety of critical situations.

Sears has gone beyond most companies in that the communications team developed, not just a template, but usable content that might be applied in future crisis situations.

As at most companies that have effective crisis plans in place, the document is shared with selected representatives from departments that might be involved in the situation and possibly included on a crisis team: the chairman, human resources, legal, finance, individual business units and the corporate ethics group.

For a crisis of any magnitude, a core crisis group (including the CEO, general counsel, and the senior vice president of public relations and communications) begins immediately to formulate the crisis response. Representatives from the rest of the company are appointed as needed; in some circumstances, the active team can include dozens of individuals from various segments of the company. The members of Sears' "external communications" staff included a director of corporate reputation and a financial media-relations expert as well as Drummond.

The crisis-plan template enumerates a fundamental step-by-step process, including:

- Team development, based on the specific expertise of individuals throughout the company

- Assignment of responsibilities and tasks

- Information development and information flow among team members during the course of a crisis

- Defining all audiences and articulating special issues or problems related to each audience.

This last step takes us well beyond process and into content and messages. For a company that, like Sears, depends on the general public for its livelihood, message development can be a gargantuan, but delicate task.

Recently, for example, Sears decided to extend employee benefits to same-sex couples. Since it has a conservative customer base, this decision could have precipitated a crisis. But the communication team was able to prepare appropriate message points in advance, which allowed Sears to support its policy without alienating its friends.

Not all potential crises become actual crises. The additional value of a well-wrought crisis plan is its flexibility. It can be useful to prepare for possible problems as well as real ones. Similarly, some problems develop slowly, and the media crisis plan can be worked over in anticipation of an expected media barrage.

The crisis plan emphasizes speed—getting the journalist to the right spokesperson fast. "There's no such thing as a news cycle anymore," says Drummond, "not when online newswires are publishing a story five minutes after something breaks."

Not being available for comment is unacceptable. A wire service will publish whatever information it has and report that the company's spokesperson could not be reached for comment. Newspapers throughout the country then pick up that report. As they reprint the wire information, they're still saying, even a week later, that the company's representative could not be reached for comment.

"There's no such thing as a news cycle anymore, not when online newswires are publishing a story five minutes after something breaks," says Jan Drummond, until recently Sears Roebuck's senior director, external communications.

Staffing is one area where Drummond sounds a different note than what we heard in Chapter 2 from Nancy Banks and Chris Hinze. For companies like theirs, media crisis experience is certainly a plus, but Drummond wants media team members who have definitely "been through the wringer."

"They must know how the media works, and they must understand what the media wants," says Drummond.

The Sears Crisis Plan in Action

Two things set Sears, Roebuck and Co. apart from most companies: One, a crisis plan has existed since 2000 that allows for immediate planning on all important fronts, including media communications. Two, Sears' in-house lawyers have an acute sense of the importance of PR and take their role in the development of a crisis response very seriously.

As a result, Sears has superior resources for incorporating input from its media communications team into a case strategy. A lawsuit the company filed against Emerson Electric provides a perfect example.

Emerson is a Sears supplier, so Sears felt the need to tread carefully in how it handled the media dimension of the litigation. On the other hand, Sears suspected what Jan Drummond, until recently Sears' senior director, external communications, describes as "active fraud" on the part of some Emerson employees.

A law department/PR department meeting focused on whether to proactively contact the press with Sears' side of the story. A working statement to the press was vetted by both departments, and Emerson's likely reactions to the statement were measured. The "business decision" was to go public proactively, as a message to Emerson that Sears was very serious about this litigation.

The combined wisdom of the legal and PR experts resulted in a compromise strategy that would put Emerson on notice, but not put Emerson in a position where it would have to lash back with all it had. This solution, says Drummond, was to call the press but "not flog the story for a week or two." She would just deliver Sears' message and then back off for a bit.

In lieu of a press release, Drummond left voice mails—it was a Friday afternoon—with her contacts at Reuters, the Associated Press and a couple of newspapers. It was a fairly big story for a few days, but then, as planned, it faded into oblivion. Sears made its point, but Emerson was left with wiggle room.

The key words: "as planned." It was an articulate strategy made possible because a crisis plan existed that put company lawyers into the same room with company PR pros at a crucial juncture in the evolving story.

They must also know when the news is going to be bad, and why you sometimes just have to swallow unfair coverage.

During the Enron scandal, for example, a reporter called with questions about Sears' off-balance-sheet assets. There is nothing wrong with companies like Sears having assets off the balance sheet, but, in the Enron environment, it was Drummond's job to manage expectations among Sears employees. Some uninformed and negative mention in the press was likely.

Such crucial internal communication doesn't happen naturally or serendipitously. It happens because there is an internal structure that allows and encourages interaction during a crisis. Again, crisis team formation and crisis plans are inseparable. The plans bring the teams into existence and the team members breathe life into the plans.

So Don't Forget...

The crisis plan is your crisis team's indispensable blueprint. It sets forth basic policies and procedures. It also allows for enough flexibility so that team members can adopt specific action points in response to specific problems. It lists the essential questions that need to be asked at the outset of any crisis. Among the plan's key elements:

- It is proactive, drawn up before a crisis. Because it is written during the calm before a storm, significant points—questions like "Should we call the media or wait for the media to call us?"—are less likely to be omitted.

- It directs team members to define all information that will be needed and how that information can be gathered. It also focuses team members on information not yet available and on where such information might be obtained.

- It assigns specific roles and responsibilities to each team member.

- It defines the vital audiences: consumers, family members of disaster victims, shareholders, etc.

- It is available, often on a Web site, to all need-to-know crisis team members, 24/7.

4

Handling the Print Interview

There are primarily two types of media that you may expect to encounter during a crisis: print and electronic. In this chapter, we'll take a look at the print media.

Message Points

The first step is to work with your media team to craft "message points."

"Where there is, or likely to be, substantial media coverage, a primer of stock phrases is not useful," says James Eiszner, head of the antitrust group at Shook, Hardy & Bacon in Kansas City, Missouri. "Careful, early work with the client and, ideally, a media specialist, is important to develop a few themes that are solidly supported and to brief spokespersons on how those themes should be delivered to the media."

These messages are the points that you must get across in no uncertain terms. They are the distilled essence of what you want to say to the world and what you want the world to believe. They communicate your key position on all the basic issues confronting you or your business in the current crisis.

Likewise important, message points keep you focused. They help you avoid volunteering distracting information that is irrelevant to your position or to what you want to get across—information that could supplant your real message points when the reporter sits down to write the story. If you don't stay on point, your digression may be the only quote from you that appears in the story.

Ideally, your message points will dominate and influence the perception of the interviewer both during the interview and afterward. At the very least, they will be credible enough to make it more difficult for reporters to publish negative facts and opinions about you without feeling the need to add some balance or equivocation.

Practice your message points continually until you are able to enunciate them without sounding as if you've memorized them. The more a part of your consciousness these message points become, the better you'll be able to use them to buttress your response to a broad array of questions.

The sidebar (on the following page) offers sample message points related to one of the most notorious media crises in recent history—the Catholic Church sex scandals. Note two things about them.

First, they're relatively brief. True, you may need to elaborate on additional details during an interview. But you should always return to your message points— "bridge" back to them, as we discuss below. In all interviews, don't forget how important it is to repeat message points. By going back to them, you virtually force reporters to include in their coverage what you believe are the most important points.

Second, they are matter-of-fact—as simple and declarative as possible. You do not want to be argumentative or defensive or exhortatory. The key is to stay on track, not to be carried away by your own emotion or conviction.

You will want to confer with your media team to determine the tone with which you deliver the message points. "Matter-of-fact" should not mean bland. Some message points ought to be delivered—not argumentatively—but passionately.

Imagine a businesswoman who, after three decades of unimpeachable professional integrity, is suddenly and unjustly accused of stealing. To be effective, the message point refuting the charge should be delivered with the simple conviction, dignity and power that anyone would expect of someone in this position.

This businesswoman can underscore basic declarative points with restrained but palpable emotion. For example: "Not once in thirty years has anyone accused me of impropriety. Not once has anyone brought such allegations to my attention privately. Suddenly, I am being publicly accused of impropriety. I am profoundly disappointed that someone would choose to make these allegations in this manner."

The content of the message point includes two forceful elements: past innocence, and the odd fact that no one

Sample Message Points: A Church Under Siege

No media-feeding in recent years has been more frenzied than the response to the sex scandals endured by the Catholic Church. It is an unfortunate example of what happens when an institution does not have consistent message points in place in preparation for use throughout a crisis—message points that, despite the size and complexity of the institution, could cohere from Rome to Dublin to Boston.

Here is a sample of the kind of effective messaging that was used successfully at one point and would have likewise well served all affected Archdioceses and Orders.

1. Our hearts go out to all victims of sexual abuse, and we are fully available to anyone who has been victimized. We will cooperate fully with civil authorities as they undertake their investigations, and we will impose all appropriate punitive measures on our end.

2. If individuals are found to have been innocent, it is our hope that you will join us in exonerating these people as zealously and as persistently as they have been accused and investigated.

3. Because allegations of misdoing are now so rife and highly publicized, we must be doubly vigilant to protect innocent clergy who may be accused—especially as, in this atmosphere, disturbed individuals, or malevolent individuals, may see an opportunity to lodge false but damaging allegations.

Notice that the message points above do not include an expression of confidence that the investigation will fully vindicate the accused. In fact, attorneys counsel against that message. "The most helpful comment is that your client is 'cooperating fully with the investigation,'" advises William Sampson, a partner in the Overland Park, Kansas, office of Shook, Hardy & Bacon, and as of this writing, the incoming president of DRI (Defense Research Institute, the primary organization of and resource for law firms representing corporate defendants in litigation).

By contrast, "expressing confidence that the investigation will vindicate the client may antagonize the prosecutor, who will then be less inclined to negotiate with you if the investigation does turn up something," according to Sampson, who defends white-collar criminal as well as civil cases.

brought the situation to her attention except in a sudden, public context. It thus shifts the moral burden back onto the shoulders of the accuser.

And, there is clear room for strategic emotion.

Reporters are usually human, and they are impressed by passion if it is measured and intelligent. Note that the repetition of the phrase "Not once" allows for emphasis in the delivery. It is a rhetorical device that communicates logic combined with righteous force.

You may need to craft message points that acknowledge a painful truth that you simply cannot talk around. Especially in a business context that does not involve malfeasance but does involve a serious economic setback, be straight with the journalist. At the same time, develop message points that can ameliorate the perception of crisis or even suggest positive dimensions.

"We all recognize that many [business] situations are not black and white," comments Rick Schmitt, a legal reporter for the *Los Angeles Times*, based in that newspaper's Washington, D.C., bureau. (Schmitt is also a veteran legal reporter for other leading publications, including *The Wall Street Journal*.) "There are always shades of gray" that can be used to balance the story.

Let's say four partners have just left your law firm and taken $10 million in business to a competitor. "Maybe it's just as well they left," says Schmitt. "Maybe they have a history of jumping firms."

And—just maybe—the other firms they left have also prospered in the intervening years. Or, adds Schmitt, maybe there were cultural incompatibilities that actually reflect well on your firm, if, for instance, your firm is a very collegial, cooperative place, and the departing partners are 900-pound gorillas who must have everything their way all the time.

Don't deny the $10 million loss or pretend it won't sting. But emphasize in your message points a persistent reason why the reporter and his or her readers will be sympathetic and even want to root for you in the months ahead.

As Schmitt agrees, these ameliorating factors—these "shades of gray"—may wind up taking up more space in the article than the specific adverse event.

Finally, no matter how bad the crisis, there may always be an opportunity to deal with it in a way that accentuates a positive—so much so, perhaps, that the ultimate effect of the media crisis is to enhance your reputation to an extent where it's even stronger than before the crisis began.

A single strategic message point may sometimes accomplish this happy reversal. In the late 1990s, a partner at a major law firm had stolen millions and was able to get away with it because his particular practice was so esoteric that no one detected the thievery.

The firm's message point was this: "As most major law firms continue to grow and add on abstruse specialties, it becomes harder for anyone to feel totally safe." The second part of the message point was the coup de grace that deflected the whole issue well beyond the firm itself, even as it underscored the essential integrity of the firm. Message: "If it can happen here, it can happen anywhere." (See Chapter 10 for more on this salient law firm media success.)

Bridging Over Troubled Waters

Watch the world's successful politicians. No matter what reporters ask them, they always find a way to conclude their answers by repeating whatever point is in their interest to make.

> "We all recognize that many [business] situations are not black and white," comments Rick Schmitt, a legal reporter for the Los Angeles Times, based in that newspaper's Washington, D.C., bureau. "There are always shades of gray" that can be used to balance the story.

"Senator, do you deny that you stole $25,000?"

"I do deny it, and I am sure that the special prosecutor's report will vindicate me so that I can get back to the job that the people of my great state elected me to do—which is to reduce taxes. It is so important that we get a fair tax and that we not burden America's businesses and entrepreneurs with bloated government spending."

"Senator, are you worried about Suzie Johnson testifying that she saw you steal the money?"

"The special prosecutor will evaluate all testimony for what it's worth, assuming it's worth anything. I have full faith in the special prosecutor and that the justice system will take its course so that we can return to the real

business of the United States Senate, which is to reduce
taxes. It is so important that we get a fair tax and..."

In a corporate or personal crisis, it is essential to direct the flow of dialogue as much as possible. Our senator quoted above may be a disingenuous rascal, but his technique is sound. Bridge back to your message points at all times. At best, it will get the reporter off some nagging detail that will distract him or her from the essential message that you want to get across. At the least, it will provide one more opportunity for you to remind the reporter what the message is.

Bridging thus allows you to influence the main theme of an article that is being written about you, rather than waiting around to see which ancillary detail—a detail that may be damaging, and is certainly not important to your purposes in any event—the reporter chooses to spotlight.

Along with your message points, work with your media team on a hypothetical Q&A that incorporates the messages and constantly bridges back to them. See the sidebar (on the following page) for an example of how, in an ideal crisis response, the Catholic Church might have effectively bridged back to one or more basic message.

Message points are the heart and soul of how to communicate with the media during a crisis. Hang them on the wall where you can clearly see them while you're talking on the phone.

At the same time, there are a number of best practices —necessary best practices—that should hang right alongside the message points. These are rules to live by in a crisis.

Brevity is the soul of wit

Don't be afraid to keep your mouth shut after you make your point to a reporter. One inveterate trick that sly reporters use, especially in a phone interview, is to say nothing after you finish talking. A full 30 seconds might go by before they get to their next question. Their scheme is to make you feel uncomfortable enough to nervously blurt out something you shouldn't say.

Sample Q&A: Setting the Agenda Yourself

Here's how the Catholic Church might have "bridged" to simple and eloquent message points, despite unpredictable questions designed to lure the interviewees into making perilous extraneous comment.

Q: *Tell me something, why do so many priests get in trouble?*

A: As a non-Catholic sociologist at Penn State, Phillip Jenkins, has documented, sexual abuse is no more common among priests than among any other group in society. Clearly, though, we need to be more open to discussing the pressures and temptations they face on a day-to-day basis, even as we need to have a zero-tolerance policy for priests who give in to the worst of those temptations. If individuals are found to have been innocent, it is our hope that you will join us in exonerating these people as zealously and as persistently as they have been accused and investigated.

Q: *What of the allegation that accused priest John Doe has a "split personality?"*

A: We don't engage in speculation about what's in others' minds, and we expect the same in return. If we uncover misdeeds, we will take all appropriate punitive measures, including summary dismissal from the Order. We have only known Father Doe to be an inspiring, loving, demanding and respectful pastor. Just as it is difficult to imagine the pain of sexual abuse, so too is it difficult to imagine the horror of being wrongfully accused of such a misdeed.

Q: *What about all the dossiers that our sources say they sent to the Vatican, and which never once generated a response?*

A: No one has ever seen these dossiers except the people who allegedly wrote them. We don't know what's in them; we don't even know they really exist. You can't condemn a human being on the basis of secret dossiers that no one's seen. That's Orwellian. That offends common decency. If individuals are found to have been innocent, it is our hope that you will join us in exonerating these people as zealously and as persistently as they have been accused and investigated. Just as it is difficult to imagine the pain of sexual abuse, so too is it difficult to imagine the horror of being wrongfully accused of such a misdeed.

Disclose all (usually)

Yes, be brief in your responses, but comprehensive in covering the bases. Don't let the reporters find out something for themselves. Take a cue from prosecutors who during a trial will reveal a plea bargain before the defense side has a chance to do so. Reporters will likely find out what you don't want them to know anyway, and then come back and confront you with the information, loaded for bear. By telling them yourself, you minimize the impact of the information.

No "no comments"
Pre-Enron studies showed that 62 percent of Americans equated "no comment" with "we're guilty." The numbers have only gone up since Enron. "No comment" concedes the entire story to the opposing point of view and possibly even communicates indifference.

"Many executives and a lot of lawyers share the same personality disadvantage, and that is the need to maintain absolute control," observes litigator Howard Scher, a partner in the Philadelphia office of Buchanan Ingersoll. "We have customarily equated absolute control with saying 'no comment' whenever confronted by the media.

"It is a dangerously unsophisticated way to deal with a media inquiry," adds Scher. "We can and should provide information that won't come back to haunt us if we're careful about it. We can also learn something about our own cases—both how the public (and potential jurors) perceive it, and what our opponents are thinking—by engaging in an ongoing dialogue with the media. 'No comment' actually means less, not more control."

Paint when you talk
All the great communicators win their points by making them in a way that people can see. Remember the hanging chads in the Florida election…those visible entities told a story that made the opposition look ridiculous. On the other hand, there was no equally vivid picture in the Democratic complaint that African-Americans were being disenfranchised. As a result, George W. Bush became President of the United States.

Be human
Small things go a long way. For instance, use the reporter's first name during the interview. Establishing personal contact lessens the chance the reporter will take a cheap shot or publish something negative that isn't absolutely substantiated.

Message Point Support:
Harnessing a Groundswell of Goodwill

Among the best practices for developing and delivering message points, you may sometimes find a most effective weapon at your disposal, even in situations doused in controversy. It's called third-party endorsement—a thunderous affirmation of your point and of your client's credibility by an outside party that may be so powerful as to sweep all press coverage in your direction.

Here is an example: When litigator Christopher Caldwell and his firm, Los Angeles' Caldwell, Leslie, Newcombe & Pettit, began representing Dr. Paul Fleiss, father of accused Hollywood madam Heidi Fleiss, it was "late in the game," as Caldwell recalls. Charges of falsely cosigning a home loan for his daughter had already been filed against the prominent pediatrician. (He stipulated that he would be occupying the house, which was not the case.) It was an "outrageous" attempt by the prosecutor to use Dr. Fleiss to pressure Ms. Fleiss into a plea bargain, according to Caldwell.

Dr. Fleiss eventually pled out and kept his license. And the judge publicly questioned the prosecutor's tactics. That questioning was duly noted in the press. Yet the *caliente* nature of the story was such that media mismanagement might have still wounded Dr. Fleiss' reputation and caused immense personal pain.

Fortunately, that reputation was the best resource for Caldwell. Fleiss was a veritable "saint," a doctor who tended to the poor, and from some of those patients "took vegetables for payment" in lieu of money, as Caldwell puts it. Over 700 letters in praise of Dr. Fleiss were gathered. Approximately 200 mothers and children turned up in court. Remember *Miracle on 34th Street*?

Yet Caldwell took no chances. He personally talked with every reporter before he let his client do so, and then rehearsed Dr. Fleiss to ensure he would not say anything wrong. A powerful two-part message point evolved: (1) here was a selfless community servant who (2) only did for his daughter what most any father would have done. When the judge also repeated the second part of the message in open court, it was game, set and match, as far as the media was concerned.

While Caldwell was wise in his circumspection, the client did enjoy an additional, rather unusual advantage. Some reporters at the *Los Angeles Times* were parents, and their pediatrician of choice was Paul Fleiss. Nothing like a third-party endorsement from the reporter down the hall!

Know the rules

During a crisis, it is especially important to know the difference between "on the record," "off the record," and "not for attribution." Off the record means the reporters cannot print what you say in any context (although they can print it if the information is obtained through other sources or becomes public). Not for attribution means they can print it, but not name you in the process. Rare is the journalist who doesn't honor the agreement—but you must clearly set the rule before you answer a single question.

Know about the reporter

Is the journalist an investigative reporter by trade? Has he or she been tough or unfair in the past? There may not be a lot of time for a background check, but get what you can. If the reporter is a pit bull, you will have to face the grilling —but the more you know, the more you will be able to gear your comments to the reporter's level of sophistication.

There are even subtle ways to make a journalist a little more modest and affect the coverage to your advantage. Let's say you run a computer company and you're being sued for patent infringement. If you dwell on the complexity of the technical material, even sophisticated reporters may be daunted and less confident about jumping to conclusions than if they were covering a sex scandal.

Play for time

Researching the background or the reporter requires time, so don't respond to interviews just when the reporters call. Find out their deadline, and promise to get back to them early enough. Then use that breathing space to research the reporter and, if necessary, the newspaper or magazine itself. It also allows time to further rehearse or modify your message points. Always get back to them before their deadline, even if just to say that you cannot comment on this particular issue at this moment. At least you've shown a professional courtesy that will likely be appreciated.

Many of the points we've made in this chapter are equally sound whether the media involved is a newspaper or a prime-time television broadcast. But the dynamics can also be fundamentally different, depending on whether you're bring interviewed by Ben Bradlee or Ed Bradley.

That's the subject of our next chapter—knowing the difference between print and broadcast media expectations, and how, in a crisis, you need to prep differently for both.

So Don't Forget...

Once the planning and staffing of the crisis plan is completed, implementation begins. At the heart of implementation is the press interview itself. To maximize positive press coverage:

- Have succinct message points in place. These are simple, declarative statements that summarize your "case." Write them down. During phone interviews, have them in front of you.

- Repeat the message points at every possible point during the interview. "Bridge" back to them as often as possible. Don't worry that reporters may sense your reliance on this tried-and-true tactic. Repetition will still maximize the likelihood that you will be quoted in your own carefully crafted language.

- Matter-of-fact doesn't mean bland. Even the most carefully worded message point can be delivered with passion and conviction.

- Devise hypothetical Q&As to guide you during the interview. Include negative questions and come up with practicable responses.

- Work toward a relationship with reporters. A good relationship increases the chances of good coverage. Little things, like calling reporters by their first names, go a long way.

5

How Attorneys, and Their Clients, Can Survive the Broadcast Media Pit Bulls

A ll of the dangers that attorneys and their clients encounter when dealing with the print media are magnified tenfold when the television cameras are rolling.

The impact of a mistake is obviously greater because the audience is so vast. And the mistake can be replayed on the air all day long or longer if it's important or juicy enough. How many times have you seen President Clinton wag his finger in denial of sexual misconduct? Dozens of times? Hundreds?

The stakes are therefore enormous. In many instances, what happens during those three or four visual bites that run on the evening news can be a great deal more decisive for your client, and perhaps for you, than anything that happens in the courtroom.

The chances that you will be misrepresented are also greater. The television interview process does not permit the give-and-take that allows reporters to conscientiously approximate the truth in a fair news venue. There are no six-paragraph appendages qualifying the point of the story with caveats and counter-claims. There is just the raw, naked point itself. You have ten seconds to make it. Your adversary gets ten seconds too.

For attorneys, who make their living exercising control, it's the most challenging media experience imaginable— because here they have no control! They can't ask to verify direct quotes prior to a broadcast as they can with the print media. Worst of all, TV coverage is ruled by film editors who can and usually do whittle your comments down to whatever they want to run and in whatever context they want to run it. The most astute commentary can look ludicrously fatuous once it finally airs.

Alas, it's very difficult to decline a TV appearance, especially in a high-profile case when the cameramen and reporters simply show up and stick the microphone in your face. In such situations, accused criminals bury their faces in drawn-up overcoats. For the rest of us, that's not an option.

"In Illinois, the cameras are not allowed in the courtroom," says Kimball Anderson, a partner at Winston & Strawn in Chicago. "But the reporters will greet you in the hallway of the court building—and they're very good at blocking the exits!"

You may also have to go on TV because your opponent is doing so. It's a defensive measure that, if it doesn't help your client, at least minimizes the harm that television coverage inevitably causes. With TV, damage control is often the best you can hope for, answering charges by a prosecutor or opposing counsel, perhaps, or defusing rampant media speculation and fervid public gossip.

> *"Reporters will greet you in the hallway of the court building—and they are very good at blocking the exits," says Kimball Anderson, a partner at Winston & Strawn.*

On the other hand, TV is not without its potential for concrete positive gains. Richard Ben-Veniste, a partner in the Washington, D.C., office of Mayer, Brown, Rowe & Maw, believes that, if you maintain a "reasoned, temperate" demeanor in front of the camera, "avoiding bombast," you can quiet "some of the hype and frenzy," some of the Chicken Little hubbub that may surround your client, especially if the "media pack has been headed in the other direction" against you.

Ben-Veniste is a veteran of many on-air encounters with angle-hungry TV reporters. During the 1970s, he was the 29-year-old Chief of the Watergate Special Prosecutor's Office for the Department of Justice. A decade later, he represented lawyer Howard Criden, accused of setting up the payoffs in the ABSCAM scandal. And, a decade after that, he was minority counsel to the U.S. Senate in the Whitewater investigation.

Survival Tactics

"TV isn't pro-Democrat or pro-Republican," says Ben-Veniste. "It's pro-scandal."

Television reporters will more often call you—not to tap your reasoned insights on the Sarbanes-Oxley Act, or some other statutory development—but because they're on

Live from Florida...

As a momentous event—not just in American political history—but in the history of the media as well, the 2000 election recount in Florida offers myriad lessons for crisis and media managers. Because it was a TV broadcast, the lesson on visuals was spectacularly underscored. Always communicate in visuals. Always make your visuals more powerful than the other guy's.

If Democratic voters were disenfranchised, there were no visuals to back up that contention or drive it home. By contrast, the hanging chads worked powerfully for the Republicans, adding visual absurdity as a factor influencing perceptions of the Gore complaint.

Since much of the crisis was live on TV, the Florida saga also underscored the need to pick your spokespersons well. Here again, the Republicans had a decisive upper hand.

G. Irvin Terrell, a trial counsel to President Bush and Vice President Cheney during the Florida struggle, believes an important decision was to "bifurcate" the choice. Former Secretary of State James Baker would speak to policy and position, reiterating essential message points about how rules cannot be changed midstream. Baker might scoff at the Democratic position, but a second spokesperson, former Montana Governor and Republican National Chairman Marc Rocicot, would be the real attack dog.

In the war of former Secretaries of State, Baker also posed a powerful contrast to Warren Christopher, a respected spokesperson for the Democrats, but not nearly as commanding or svelte as the occasion required.

Terrell, a partner at Baker Botts in Houston and a veteran of much high-profile litigation, including the Texaco/Pennzoil case of the late 1980s, believes the Democrats relied too heavily on their attorney, David Boies, whose constant media chores may have made him "less focused" on the case itself. (Uncharacteristically, Boies did not return our repeated calls for comment.)

If so, there's a lesson here for crisis planners on how trial attorneys should be deployed during litigation, especially since Boies' easy facility with the media is often held up as a paradigm for attorneys who want to maximize their client's case as well as aggressively promote themselves. If Boies was actually part of the problem, rather than the solution, for client Al Gore, the case would certainly suggest that choice of spokesperson should never be automatic.

Is there a natural flow from advocacy in the courtroom to advocacy on the courthouse steps, where reporters, not jurors, are the arbiters? If so, the trial attorney is a natural spokesperson. If not, the strategy needs to be refined.

the trail of something that's very damaging to your client and very entertaining to their audiences. Publishers may need to sell newspapers but, with TV, we're dealing with the entertainment industry, pure and simple.

As they say in the industry, "If it bleeds, it leads."

Here is a brief catalogue of the dos and don'ts, a beginner's Prime Time Survival Manual. As we emphasize throughout these pages, media relations is more art than science. The most learned rules, including these, may therefore need to be jettisoned as circumstances develop.

1. Decline comment only with great care

Refusing comment is okay if you know for certain that your opponents—all of them, from opposing counsel to hostile on-air pundits—are going to do the same. Of course, that is not often the case. Generally, you need to say something if you can.

On the other hand, sometimes you just can't. Your case may be at a stage when any public commentary is deleterious, if not actually prohibited by the Bar rules. "Don't be bullied by the reporter," advises Ben-Veniste. Explain to them why you cannot comment "and do so with a smile."

As Ben-Veniste points out, there are additional benefits that may accrue if you stand your ground. In some situations, "if you don't comment, they just won't have anything to run. That means you've kept your client off the air for at least another day, and usually that's all to the good."

When you give reporters, even TV reporters, a credible reason why you cannot comment, you are treating them as professionals. "Create a courtroom atmosphere" in all your dealings with the media, advises criminal lawyer Albert Krieger, a frequent on-air presence as attorney in the Wedtech scandal that rocked New York City in the 1980s and, a few years later, as mobster John Gotti's counsel.

That courtroom creates ground rules for dealing with the media where there were none before. Declining comment is not then an evasion, but obedience to something bigger than all of us. "One reporter stuck a microphone in my face and asked me if I believed there was really such a thing as the Mafia," recalls Krieger.

"'Sir, there is a trial going on,' I answered, and left it at that."

The Best Ways to Say Nothing

Kimball Anderson warns that any commentary to reporters outside the courtroom opens both you, and your client, to defamation charges.

"You cannot repeat allegations," says Anderson, a partner at Winston & Strawn who represented the estate of Suzanne Olds, bludgeoned to death after a nasty divorce from her husband, Dean Olds.

Mr. Olds, one of the leading intellectual property attorneys in the country, had taken up with a young German male lover, who was charged with the murder and freed on a technicality. He then skipped the country. Dean Olds was never indicted. Anderson filed what turned out to be a successful civil suit to prevent Olds from seizing control of the dead woman's estate.

The safest course, and often the only course, is to deliver what Anderson calls "a bland factual recitation."

He also represented Illinois Governor George Ryan in his public struggle against Jim Ryan, the state attorney general, on the death-penalty clemency issue. The case would have been of great interest to TV under any circumstances, but the fact that Jim Ryan used it in his gubernatorial race guaranteed ongoing on-air coverage.

Commenting on a case to TV reporters can be a daunting and dangerous adventure. Resisting such commentary can be equally daunting, especially when you actually see your adversary spinning his or her position for the cameras. In the Olds case, "Olds himself was standing there everyday telling his side to the TV reporters," recalls Anderson. Part of the lawyer's job is to "deflect" media attention from the client, but in a way that keeps the reporters friendly while throwing them only the barest bones.

Toward that end, attorneys should usually explain the constraints that have been placed on them in a way that expresses professional respect for the reporters. The "my hands are tied" line is often the best you can do. For the majority of reporters, even TV reporters, that's usually enough. One reliable alternative strategy is to direct reporters to a disinterested third party for background or for commentary and attribution. By doing so, you've kept the reporter happy, while there's a good chance your surrogate will get your point of view across.

In the capital-punishment fracas, Anderson made a televised statement, with the governor's approval, accusing the attorney general of being politically motivated. The statement was aired throughout the daily news cycle.

2. Cut to the chase

As suggested above, a major difference between electronic- and print-media interviews is the amount of information the reporter is willing to listen to, and the amount of information that will get into the story. Print reporters have more time to put stories together, listen to interview subjects and incorporate what they learn in suitably in-depth articles. Give these reporters all you've got.

By contrast, don't fill in too much detail for electronic journalists unless asked to do so. If you are giving an interview during a "live" report situation, be aware that you may have an opportunity to get out only three or four sentences before you are cut off. So you must deliver your primary message point first and quickly move to Point Two if you can.

In any event, be ready to repeat Point One, especially if the reporter asks something like, "Is there anything else you would like to add?"

All our suggestions about bridging and about sticking to the message points, made with respect to the print media in the preceding chapter, are exponentially more crucial on television.

"Edit out all your caveats," says Anderson, "but then incorporate them into your sound bites." In other words, if the caveats are important enough to communicate at all, they should not be caveats. Rewrite your message point so everything you need to say is included there, in more or less the same number of words as the original message point.

Anderson is unusual. He has achieved a sophisticated sense of how to fashion and deliver message points without having been formally trained to do so. But media training with public relations professionals is something he considers useful, as a way to shortcut the painful learning process that most attorneys must otherwise endure face to face with both print and electronic media. Training for TV interviews should include practice before the camera. Trainees get a chance to see what they look like as their skills develop.

Effective TV appearances—featuring short, to-the-point messages—do not require a dynamic media presence. Anderson is a careful, soft-spoken man; no Gerry Spence, to be sure. As such, his on-air success is all the more relevant to most attorneys. During TV interviews, "I think carefully about what I'm going to say before I say it, and I don't worry if five or ten seconds of silence elapse.

"They're not going to run those five or ten seconds of silence anyway," he says. "They'll cut them right out."

3. Include TV in the crisis plan

Even the well-laid crisis plans, like those we looked at in Chapter 3, do not usually include the immediate steps that need to be taken if a *60 Minutes* crew shows up at the receptionist's desk. Most corporate communications departments are not experienced in this area, and they simply do not know what to do.

Consult a media-crisis expert for help formulating a plan before any crisis happens. He or she will advise you to adjust your crisis plan for TV, with specific directives to:

- Bargain for time. The longer you can delay a TV interview, the better. The plan should include the actual language that should be used during these negotiations; e.g., "Please be patient, let me know your questions, give me a number where I can reach you, and we will call you back as soon as possible. What is your deadline?"

- Pick the spokesperson with an eye toward his or her credibility and appearance. Some people just don't look sympathetic, no matter how honest they are.

- Politely ask the TV crew to leave and come back later, deadline permitting, unless a spokesperson has been chosen and prepped, and is available.

- Politely ask the TV reporters not to talk to anyone on the premises, until the proper spokesperson arrives.

- Promise more access to key people if they are cooperative. There should always be a *quid pro quo*. If your "key people" are public personalities who will increase the entertainment value of the story, then you're really talking the TV reporter's language.

- Make sure you know what kind of broadcast it is. Is it *20/20*, or the nightly news? Both may dote on scandal, but some shows depend on it. You'll need to manage reporters' expectations as a result. An investigative team doing an investigative program will invariably broadcast something negative. Be ready to take the hit.

4. Develop, maintain—and manipulate relationships

The same logic applies to TV reporters as to print reporters. If they know you, they are more likely to treat you better.

Personal relationships also let you better anticipate what's coming and provide some assurance that you're not about to get sucker-punched in front of millions of viewers. Attorneys like Ben-Veniste "always differentiate" between reporters they know and those they don't know.

Rapport comes in many packages, and in many contexts. For example, "off the record" or "not for attribution" has no meaning during TV broadcasts. You can't make some statement during a TV interview with any reasonable expectation that it will be edited out because you've asked that it be off the record.

Yet Ben-Veniste will often chat with a reporter or producer directly before a broadcast, giving them whatever background information might sway the line of questioning in his direction. Again, a potential liability in TV coverage —the fact that it is immediate and irrevocable—can be played to your benefit.

As Ben-Veniste explains, the reporter isn't going to hearken back to your previous conversation, or use it to trip you up. "He is not going to say, 'But when we chatted before the show, you said such-and-such!' That would destroy the illusion of immediacy that TV tries to convey in the interview."

If you're trapped in the electronic moment, so are they. Ben-Veniste will likewise use commercial interruptions during a program to chat pleasantly with interviewers and casually suggest fertile areas to explore when the interview resumes.

Black Hats, White Hats

To paraphrase Billy Crystal, "It is wonderful to be mah-velous but it is more wonderful to look mah-velous."

Remember, TV news, like TV cowboy shows or TV cop thrillers, requires good guys and bad guys. The good guys look like good guys. The bad guys look like bad guys.

Doing something about these crucial visual determinants—well, that's the tricky part. You can't change your face or your physique. In some instances, the better part of valor is to defer to another spokesperson as the TV point person. However, attorneys representing clients in high-profile cases don't usually have that option. It's part of their job to go on television.

One of the most respected criminal attorneys in the United States, Albert Krieger, offers a particularly interesting example of how to adjust a potentially damaging visual appearance and manner to the exigencies of the visual media. During the 1980s, he was a frequent presence on television as his client—one John Gotti—was tried and re-tried until finally convicted and sent to prison.

Krieger is squat-shouldered, bald and craggy-faced. He looks like the kind of lawyer a murderer might hire. "It was something I thought about all the time," says Krieger.

Moreover, Krieger is a zealous advocate. He has strong opinions and expresses them strongly. When we joked that he was scarier on TV than his infamous client, Krieger related that in the early 1970s, he had done a training video for an opening session of the National College of Criminal Defense. He was painstaking in his efforts to observe proper decorum and maintain professional gentility as he demonstrated the fine points of cross-examination.

When he saw the video for the first time, he was shocked by his own ferocity. "If this is what I am like when I'm trying to be gentle, what must I look like when I'm not! I lost a full night's sleep fretting over it."

Krieger's solution was a simple one: to use the English language well and earn the respect of reporters for the substance of his remarks. "No 'dees' and 'dems,' no street talk, just [substantive] legal sound bites," says Krieger. "There was nothing more I could do. With a careful use of language, I tried to moderate the [impression] I made."

Is that enough to impress a TV audience bound up wholly in the visuals? Probably not. But at least by impressing the reporters, Krieger avoided the trap that another one of Gotti's attorneys, Bruce Cutler, fell into—being portrayed by the media, not as a respectable criminal lawyer, but as a "legal mouthpiece."

There's no doubt the respect Krieger earned from the TV reporters carried over into their coverage and tempered the unsettling visual impact. Throughout the Gotti trials, you never heard a bad word about him.

5. Control the visuals. Understand their effects.

Mitigate or exploit those effects. Richard Nixon was obsessed with how he looked on television, and for good reason. His body language was naturally jagged and five-o-clock shadows adumbrated his image on TV for three decades. As best he could, President Nixon took stock of his visual assets and liabilities. So should you.

At the very least, look like you're happy to be there. One reason many athletes are PR disasters is that, when they are interviewed after a game, they look as put-upon as they feel. A more affable presence not only communicates better with the audience, it can affect how the interviewer deals with you.

"If you seem to enjoy yourself, you get a bigger break," says Barbara Sessions, director of business development at Winston & Strawn, a firm that includes a number of TV-savvy attorneys. In addition to Anderson, the firm includes former Governor James Thompson and Dan Webb, a former U.S. Attorney who's argued effectively on TV on behalf of the tobacco industry.

Cutting-Room Floor

Media relations as an art is all about exercising control. Unfortunately, with TV, the biggest problem for control-conscious attorneys is that the editing process deprives them of essential input. "They'll work you over for an hour, and then run two minutes of fluff," observes Albert Krieger.

Krieger's solution is to exercise maximum care and make absolutely certain he gives them nothing in that hour to embarrass him or hurt his client. "A good working rule is to be as painfully boring for the hour as you possibly can be," he says. Don't worry about disappointing the reporters. It's not your job, nor necessarily in your interest, to make them happy.

There are rules you can set about questions themselves, adds Krieger—not to request confidential information, not to ask judgmental questions, etc. But the editing process, the transformation from interview to program, is altogether beyond your oversight.

Ben-Veniste has relied on a simple approach: He only does live broadcasts. Over the years these have included a dozen *Larry King Live* and the Sunday morning network news programs. But he scrupulously avoids the cable TV shouting matches. There's simply nothing to be gained, for himself or his clients, by participating in these interminable ideological squabbles.

A live interview provides a powerful forum that's even safer than the most respectable print outlets. You can't be misquoted. You can't be taken out of context. It's just you and Larry King, so you sink or swim on your merits alone.

So Don't Forget...

The rules on TV are very different, and the process considerably more dangerous. Here are three fundamental lessons for surviving broadcasts and narrowcasts:

- Refuse to comment only if you have an airtight reason to do so that actually makes you look better in the process.

- Don't elucidate substantive points for the TV cameras. No one cares. No one will get to see them anyway. Master the art of the sound bite.

- Measure the visual impact of your appearance on television. It's a visual medium. One ugly scowl can undo volumes of verbal truth.

6

The Family Jewels: Media Strategies in Product Liability Crises

M ajor product cases can generate more media attention, with more serious consequence, than just about any other species of litigation—including the front-page corporate scandals like those that rocked the world in the summer of 2002. Those scandals will continue to fuel news columns for months and years to come, but not everyone in the world worked for Enron or Andersen or WorldCom or lived in communities decisively affected by the malfeasance.

On the other hand, if a Tylenol bottle is poisoned, if a Pinto blows up, if an airplane manufacturer sells faulty parts, anyone anywhere can be affected at any time. That sells newspapers.

Attorneys and public relations specialists deal generally with two types of product liability cases that usually require contrasting PR strategies. In the first type, the goal is to keep the product's reputation intact or to even improve its reputation—to fend off, both in a court of law and in the media, any imputation that the product is defective or dangerous.

In the second type, the product has become indefensible. It's either off the market or will be soon. Often, as with asbestos, the client is immersed in mass-tort litigation, and fundamentally different rules therefore pertain. Even the general rule of never saying "no comment," and always returning a reporter's phone call, might no longer apply.

Media and crisis management are equal parts art and science. Even the basic rules are made to be broken.

Preserving Marketplace Integrity

Let's look first at product liability cases where the clear goal is to defend the product and ensure continued marketplace viability.

Develop a theme

Once the lawsuit is filed, the first task is the most important one: Develop a theme. This theme is essentially the same message for the press as for the jury, although, for the jury, the theme usually gets presented in both long and short form.

The long form encompasses myriad supporting facts, including technical facts, rendered in language easily comprehensible to the laity. The short form is the bare message itself minus accompanying detail. It is usually repeated in court, before and during summation, to ensure the jury gets the message in its unmistakable essence.

That short form is the one to use with the media. Sometimes the trade press will want more elaborate material, if, for instance, it's an automotive publication read by industry professionals conversant with the specific workings of an internal-combustion engine. Generally, though, the evening news wants only a reasoned assertion that the product is a sound one.

The theme is the final distilled result of intense reading, knowledge of the product's history, numerous conversations with the client, and an intimate familiarity with how the product is marketed. The delivery of the theme by a lawyer or company spokesperson is all the more credible and powerful as a result of such informed comprehension.

Anne Kimball, a partner at Chicago's Wildman Harrold, who has represented the gun, alcohol, food and pharmaceutical industries, among others, offers a typical "theme" in a case involving the involuntary discharge of a firearm:

> The gun is built to discharge only when the trigger is pulled, and there is no possible way anyone can demonstrate that it discharges under any other circumstance. Mr. Jones may not have wanted to pull the trigger, but pull it he did. It's unfortunate, but there is no other possible explanation.

"Themes" are not quite the same as the "message points" discussed in Chapter 4. Message points are effective in dealing with the press, but they may not be exculpatory. In the Catholic Church crisis, for example, the message points may suggest the potential innocence of the accused, but go on to declare that, if there is evidence of misconduct, the Church will cooperate with civil authorities to the fullest extent.

The theme in a product liability case includes no such promise. It is an unqualified assertion that the product belongs on the market. It wins acquittals in courts of law and in the court of public opinion.

Restrict the battlefield

Justice, however, is not really blind. Themes in product liability cases are subject to intervening variables. Since these cases affect the welfare of every voter in the country, they are often filed with political motives resolutely in tow.

Jurors, conditioned by their own political sensibilities, often ignore irrefutable facts supporting the defense theme. How much more so the millions of consumers who are not charged by a judge or obliged to follow any rules in making their determinations about the safety of a product!

For the gun industry, for example, politics and product liability are linked inextricably. NRA hardball has further politicized these cases for many citizens. If gun control advocates can't beat the lobbyists in the legislatures, they will do so in court.

In the last few years, Anne Kimball has been defending a spate of cases filed by municipalities against her firearms industry clients. She's won most of them, and she's done so by relying on a second, supporting "theme:"

> *A court of law is not the place to determine who should and should not have access to firearms. The regulation of the firearms industry is a matter for you, as citizens, to take up with your representatives in Congress or your local legislatures. The integrity of our judicial system depends on your not confusing the issues. The issue here is simply whether or not the gun exploded, all by itself, in Mr. Jones' face.*

Humanize the Defendant,
Humanize the Spokesperson

It would seem that any product defense starts off at a disadvantage on the PR front. At best, the company is in the unenviable position of having to show the world that a product essential to its business does not cause grievous injury or death. At worst, there is a widespread if baseless presumption of guilt.

"Anyone defending a corporation these days is starting off at a disadvantage, in any kind of case," comments Anne Kimball, a litigator at Wildman Harrold with decades of experience defending high-risk industries. There's always been bias against powerful, "impersonal" business interests. Post-Enron, the bias is proportionately harder and faster.

The strategic response is a veritable best practice among product liability attorneys everywhere—humanize the corporation! That means…

- For court appearances, pick corporate representatives the jurors can relate to. Show that, if you deal unjustly with the company, you unjustly penalize the good person sitting before you in the witness box or at the defendant's table. Remember that the ear defers to the eye, so pick folks who look sympathetic as well. The more avuncular, the better.

- For media appearances, likewise pick spokespersons who sound human when they talk, and who don't sound as if they've memorized formal corporate statements. For TV appearances, sympathetic-looking spokespersons are, again, worth their weight in gold.

- For both court and media appearances, humanize the company by humanizing its legal counsel. "I'm a mother of four, stepmother of two, and grandmother of five, and I don't mind using that fact to help my client," says Kimball. "I was born in Brooklyn and I grew up on the South Side of Chicago. I know more than most people what the terror of violence is all about."

For complex product cases, Kimball has also found a way to make sure she's communicating with the world in a way the world can understand: She rehearses arguments for her family and friends. If they can understand her, chances are that jurors and reporters will too.

With reporters, she speaks slowly and often repeats herself to make sure her points get across. "I don't worry if I don't stay on the reporter's point," she says. "It's not the reporter's question that will help the case. It's my answer."

"Plaintiffs' lawyers are getting their messages to reporters well before they file suit," says Anne Kimball, a litigator at Chicago's Wildman Harrold. "So you've got to act fast. It's got to be part of the initial case strategy."

It's much tougher to de-politicize politically charged cases in the press than in court. "It depends on the journalist," says Kimball. "Sometimes they're listening to you, sometimes they're not." But you should still explicitly remind reporters that your case is one issue, and that the law of the land is another.

Different products create different issues in our politically correct and sensitive society—whether the products are SUVs, fatty foodstuffs or supplements taken by athletes. Again and again, Kimball must argue for separation of powers. She must point out that politically motivated plaintiffs ought to be taking their cases to Congress and, if Congress wants to further regulate how certain products are marketed, it is free to do so. In the gun litigation, she began making that point to the media early on, in anticipation of fervid media interest in these cases.

There are thus two strategic imperatives for the defense in many product cases. First, affirm the safety of the product. Second, keep the discussion as disinterested as possible, in and out of the courtroom.

Fine-tune the themes

Defense themes vary from industry to industry. For clients in the alcohol industry, the typical theme developed by litigators like Kimball emphasizes numbers:

> *Alcohol is responsibly consumed by millions of Americans every day. Those who abuse it represent a small minority and should be helped. The alcohol industry is heavily regulated and has responded to initiatives to minimize the damage its product can cause. There is no just reason to fault the industry for the problems of a small number of abusers, especially in light of industry initiatives to encourage responsible consumption.*

Technical Data Plus Credible Spokesperson Equals Effective Message

When you transform scientific data into a quotable sound bite, it is critical to recruit the ideal spokesperson to deliver the message. The operative principle is credibility. No volume of technical esoterica, however supportive, can replace credibility in product liability cases or in any case where the decisive testimony depends on understanding complex fact patterns.

Assume your message is: "We do not have any credible evidence of a relationship between the diet pill manufactured by my client and the plaintiff's heart disease. We can, however, demonstrate, by referencing credible medical information, that the plaintiff's heart disease is more likely related to many other risk factors."

That message has been refined from volumes of medical and scientific information submitted as evidence. To remain credible, however, it must survive assault after assault in which opposing counsel can return to any or all of the specific technical data points as a challenge to your message.

The defense must therefore rely on a fine "balance" between the simplified message and the comprehensive research that supports it, according to Ted Dunkelberger. He is senior director, product defense, at THE WEINBERG GROUP in Washington, D.C. Such consulting groups are in the business of ensuring that all the technical material has been collected and analyzed, that it supports the message in every particular and that it is effectively presented for public consumption.

Toward these ends, the consultants work with the trial lawyers to develop powerful demonstrative evidence—from simple graphics to more advanced visual displays—that complements the expert's presentation. Often, however, their most critical contribution is in expert witness identification. Ultimately the jurors, for all their conscientious efforts, may not be sure that the technical data really does support the message—unless they trust the messenger.

THE WEINBERG GROUP conducts systematic searches and interviews to identify experts with the proper credentials and skills. They consider a variety of factors to determine the expert's suitability, from testimonial history and professional presentations to appearances in the media. The ultimate goal is the recruitment of a highly credentialed expert who exudes objectivity.

The theme plays well, mainly because the public already believes it. Alcohol manufacturers and distributors have indeed been historically amenable to regulation, while a significant percentage of the public does, in fact, drink responsibly every day. In Kimball's experience, alcohol clients are usually vindicated, legally and in the media, even in tragic drunk-driving cases.

For clients defending medical devices, Kimball describes a few themes to play for jurors and reporters:

- Acknowledge that most medical devices have attendant risk.

- Emphasize the fact that the government has approved the product. Unlike other products, "you already have a strong tribunal on your side when you defend medical devices," says Kimball. "People know the FDA and people instinctively trust it."

- Underscore the positive health benefits of the product.

Once the themes are developed, espouse them early and often. "Plaintiffs' lawyers are getting their messages to reporters well before they file suit, and they often hang out in the same bars the reporters do," says Kimball. "So you've got to act fast. It's got to be part of the initial case strategy."

Preserving a Delicate Balance

If your client happens to be Owens Corning, forget most of what you've just learned.

Mass-tort litigation invariably presents a different public relations burden. In this species of product litigation, liability has often already been established. Now the issue is: How much liability? Also, there are often thousands of cases filed against your client, often with different legal counsel handling different cases in different jurisdictions.

Curb thy tongue

In mass-tort litigation, "any comments you make about your case can directly affect every other case of the same nature that involves your client in ways that can be extremely damaging," advises Mark Goodman, a partner at Debevoise & Plimpton in New York.

So you don't just trot out a few message points and deliver them at will. Often, the best thing to say, even after you've won a case, is "no comment."

Example: In July, you win a case that's part of a mass-tort litigation and you crow about it to the press. In August, your client loses the same kind of case, with the same claims and the same fact pattern, in a different jurisdiction. Now the jury retires to decide on punitives.

As Goodman points out, the plaintiff can then show your earlier press statements to the jurors for their consideration. Your gleeful expostulation sounds to them like gloating. You seem so pleased to be evading responsibility, to be literally getting away with murder.

The jurors aren't going to let you get away with it this time. They'll right the wrong by tacking on an extra $50 million or so in punitive damages.

Without seasoned legal and public relations counsel, it can get even worse.

> In mass-tort litigation, "any comments you make about your case can directly affect every other case of the same nature that involves your client, in ways that can be extremely damaging," advises Mark Goodman, a partner at Debevoise & Plimpton.

Goodman, who has represented clients like Owens Corning in a variety of mass-tort cases, offers another very bad case scenario. Assume all you do is to innocently inform the press that a case you litigated just settled for a mere $25,000. Considering the exposure in the case, that would seem a result you'd want the media to trumpet at full blast.

Yet that simple disclosure can "implicate your accounting procedures," as Goodman puts it, actually devaluing the company itself even as it attracts unwanted SEC scrutiny. Corporations must report reserve funds for contingency liability and they use a dollar amount average to calculate what they report. That average may be based on a combination of very high numbers and very low ones.

When you tell the press that a case settled for $25,000, the analysts will do a little simple arithmetic using $25,000 as a basis for evaluating the entire reserve. The company may, in fact, be sufficiently reserved, but the one settlement figure you disclosed befuddles subsequent calculations and creates a perception of underfunding.

Results: Stock values plummet and the regulators come knocking at your door. Now it's not just a question of your client paying more. Your client is suddenly worth much less.

Craft the message

In a gun case or a medical device case, the goal may be to keep the product viable. An aggressive media campaign serves that purpose. By contrast, in a mass-tort product case, the first task at hand is to mandate vows of silence among all corporate spokespersons—and to fashion a PR campaign that supports a sound legal strategy.

What should that PR campaign look like? What message point or theme can the media mavens roll out on behalf of a company that may be in Chapter 11, that is still litigating thousands of lawsuits, and that has been adjudged liable for manufacturing and marketing a deadly product a quarter of a century ago?

Goodman, using asbestos as an example, articulates a message point acknowledging some liability:

> We are not defending the conduct of the company in the past, and we are not trying to minimize the damages suffered by claimants. We will compensate everyone who has suffered asbestos-related damages as a result of our business activities. But we will also fight hard legally to ensure that we are not held responsible for false claims, for damages that are not asbestos-related, or for damages unrelated to the manufacturing and marketing of asbestos by this company.

Fashioned thus, the messaging avoids two pitfalls...

- The company is not commenting on behavior that dates back two or three decades. As Goodman points out, that's a fight the defendant won't likely win, especially in the press. Plaintiffs' attorneys can always find ways to cast aspersions on business decisions made so long ago, in a dramatically different business context. In the media, of course, reporters needn't offer any real proof.

- The company is not trying to mitigate its liability by saying that asbestos was universally thought to be a good product in the past. True or not, the point simply won't wash in today's media. The far better tack is to accept responsibility rather than argue about ancient perceptions regarding a product that turned out to be a bad one.

Having uttered the *mea culpa* for past actions and inactions, the company can now complement contrition with a positive and socially useful stated goal. Goodman's next message point:

> *It is essential that we protect ourselves from liability that is not ours, because it is our goal to make sure that we have sufficient reserves to compensate everyone who is justly entitled to compensation from us. Only by challenging unjust liability can we guarantee a just outcome for the many people who have suffered in this situation.*

The fact that 130 million people were actually exposed to asbestos, while 200 million people claimed to have been, supports the message on factual economic grounds. But such messaging also suggests the possibility of a public opinion swing. Stories that have been largely negative in the past can eventually present the client in a positive light.

For products that, unlike asbestos, are still marketable, such a turnaround should be an abiding objective of corporate crisis planning. After all, the corporate purpose is to sell the product. A mere acquittal in a court of law is a Pyrrhic victory if, despite the findings of a jury, the public still has vague misgivings.

In our next chapter, we will look at a peculiar species of product liability crisis management that requires separate consideration, as it's all about a war that's been raging for decades and may well rage on for decades to come.

So Don't Forget...

Here are five simple rules to guide media strategy during a product liability crisis...

- Focus your theme. The same story you tell to the jury, you can tell to the press. Base the theme on solid research and incontrovertible fact, but keep it simple, simple, simple.

- Watch your back. Product cases are often politically motivated or assume political significance. Take the bull by the horns with themes and message points that encourage impartiality even among partisan observers.

- Put on a human face. Jurors love corporate spokespersons who remind them of Walter Cronkite. Ditto TV audiences.

- Vary the messages. Different industries require different messages, as do different kinds of cases.

- The same simple assertion that benefits your client in a single case can be disastrous when the client is simultaneously litigating ten thousand similar cases.

7

The Road Not Taken:
Lessons from the Tobacco Wars

A major theme running through these pages is the need for control in media management. You need a plan, and you need to follow it. You need crafted messages, and you need to reiterate them. You need designated spokespersons, and you need to rely on them.

That said, the plan itself has to be a good one, the messages have to be effective, and the spokespersons have to be good.

Sound obvious? In hindsight, common sense is always obvious. Yet for two decades, experienced, aggressive communications professionals, haunting the hallways of the tobacco companies, floundered in their efforts to implement a coherent plan or articulate effective messages or deploy persuasive spokespersons.

One can't be dismissive of them or contemptuous of their apparent failures. They were up against passionate adversaries and effective communicators, not to mention legal exposure that was hard to gauge. The dangers posed by any misstep could be enormous. To be over-responsive in the media might have incited an accelerated legal and PR assault from their opponents. To be silent, on the other hand, would have conceded defeat.

Our purpose isn't to castigate those efforts, but to glean a few fundamental lessons.

First, the mistakes that the tobacco industry made did not merely vitiate its attempts to save face in public or strengthen upcoming case strategies. They were mistakes that destroyed its credibility and continue to haunt the industry today.

The biggest mistake was in letting tobacco be the issue. The industry seemed ready to fall on its sword in defense of its indefensible product. During the Waxman Committee hearings of the early 1990s, every CEO of every major tobacco company publicly swore that tobacco was not a health hazard.

By refusing to acknowledge that tobacco is very much a health hazard, the industry fostered a pandemic distrust that will dog its attempts to communicate from now till the 22nd century. The most dangerous consumer product on the market anywhere in the world is not tobacco, but alcohol. No alcohol company has dreamed of denying it. As a result, the industry has never gotten into serious trouble and the purveyors of strong spirits are trusted by the public.

Had the tobacco industry acknowledged the dangers of the product, it could have moved on early in the game to other messages—about individual choice, about confiscatory government policy, about responsibilities to shareholders and employees. But there was the fear of legal exposure in making any such admission, since there were reams of documents suggesting corporate efforts to suppress health data as far back as the 1950s. Any acknowledgement in 1994 of the dangers of tobacco could have meant a whopping lawsuit because of something that happened decades earlier.

Nonetheless, there were also reams of indisputable scientific evidence that, from a PR standpoint, made their obstinate defense of tobacco totally preposterous. The companies have backed off in recent years and now acknowledge the perils of tobacco, but it may be too late. Having tried to foist an untenable proposition on the public, it is now very difficult for them to speak the truth and be heard.

A second lesson is all about control. The industry did not control communication; often it simply stifled it. Corporate "communications" staffers put reporters through a labyrinthine process to secure interviews and often did not return calls at all. Other corporations in other industries are similarly over-controlled, administratively. But for any company that is being accused of wholesale unresponsiveness, putting up a bureaucratic maze only confirms the worst that is being said.

Yet the tobacco industry clearly did have the resources in place to do better. There were industry voices that were passionate and honest in the belief that the industry was being unfairly targeted and that there was a substantive case to make in the court of public opinion.

Had the industry relied on such voices, it would at

least have been perceived as human. And that's always a good start.

To learn a little about what the tobacco wars have to teach us, let's listen to one of those voices.

A Corporate Paralysis

Dan Donahue is senior vice-president and deputy general counsel of the R.J. Reynolds Tobacco Company. He sounds very much as he sounded when we happened to speak to him on a tobacco-related issue in the early 1990s. He is affable, he believes in what he says, he respects other people's opinions and he knows how to deliver a message point.

In short, he's the kind of spokesperson an industry wants for media outreach. An industry that is being demonized should want spokespersons to be unmistakably human. The reporter may not agree with him or her, but will hear a human voice full of concern, conviction and—not just corporate self-interest—but principle as well.

We're back to the quintessential lesson of all product liability cases, which is to humanize the corporation. Only here, the need for the human voice isn't just to win a case, but to reverse public judgment of an entire industry.

As an in-house litigator, Donahue has spoken to the press about important cases, working with a team of in-house PR advisors to hone message points and refine their delivery. If Donahue has been easier to reach than most tobacco lawyers, it's probably because the Reynolds communications staff is relatively small. He doesn't remember a planning session attended by more than four or five people. There were never a lot of people running unnecessary interference.

It was never the apparent policy of any tobacco company to encourage effective spokespersons to take the lead in getting the company's messages across to the press. Their best spokespersons were usually reactive to the events the media were calling about. The messages, however sound, were often delivered defensively as a result. The tobacco industry as a whole did not proactively seek media exposure until 1997–1998, in response to the campaigns mounted by the state attorney general.

The Essential Messages

The tobacco industry may never be able to make good on its past mistakes. Had it resolved decades ago to acknowledge the dangers of smoking (assuming such acknowledgement was legally viable), it could have hammered home key points that would have made it more sympathetic and credible.

In fact, the crucial message points—powerful, persuasive message points—were at the tip of the collective corporate tongue throughout the tobacco wars. By 1997, the industry finally moved away from its defense of smoking and would harp instead on these strong substantive points. The question is, was it too late?

First, the now-commonplace position that...

- Smoking is a matter of individual choice. We do believe that all adults have the right to smoke and that they have ample information with which to make that decision. Remember, this product is legal to produce and legal to distribute.

And then, to underscore the situation of the industry in proper context...

- The tobacco industry is not a Goliath confronting near-defenseless Davids. Quite to the contrary, there are powerful interest groups lobbying against us in Washington and in the media. Expert witnesses are generating millions in income testifying against us.

- The tobacco industry has a solemn obligation to its shareholders to be profitable. Were we to abandon that responsibility, we would face shareholder suits in every jurisdiction in this country. We have a similar responsibility to our employees to be profitable.

- It is simply wrong for the government to pursue litigation that will drive the tobacco industry out of business. We are willing to comply with reasonable safeguards protecting minors, and we want to advise the public as to the dangers of smoking. Government lawsuits amount to a confiscatory tax that no other industry has ever faced in this country.

- Today, the government has targeted the tobacco industry. Tomorrow, it will target some other industry. Will it be your industry on the receiving end as the government seeks to empty some other deep pocket?

During one conversation with a reporter in the early 1990s, Donahue followed up an answer to a question by musing, "You know, I'm probably going to get in trouble for talking to you."

Donahue remains ambivalent about how to handle the alleged misdeeds of the past. He is defensive of the corporate fathers who built, and then nearly unbuilt, RJR. He eschews any position or message point that would cast them as dishonest or irresponsible. He adds that the "jury is still out" on whether public perceptions might now improve as the big tobacco companies own up to past errors.

Donahue is likewise dubious that any coherent campaign in the past could have been effective enough in light of the circumstances.

"It's not apparent what we should have done," he says. The other side had immense media advantages. Take, for instance, the infamous photograph that confirmed a generation of distrust as only a visual image can. As the CEOs were sworn in before the Waxman Committee, they all raised their arms and swore to tell the truth. Then they said that cigarettes are not health hazards. The result was a picture reminiscent of the Nuremberg trials.

Meanwhile, plaintiffs' lawyers were leaking documents to the press in masterly fashion. The documents would generally arrive on a reporter's desk at around 3:30 pm. The tobacco companies would get a call for comment at around 4:30, with little time before deadline to respond.

As Donahue sees it, "reporters felt compelled to play up the contents of every document," for fear that, "if they didn't, they'd be dropped from the plaintiffs' [media] list" and miss out on something later on that might be really important.

To have mounted an effective counter-campaign would have required a different kind of crisis team than what the tobacco industry was willing to empower—a team respond-ing *at once* to every media inquiry with either factual material to counter accusations or a plausible explanation why some ostensible past misdeed was irrelevant to an ongoing case or to the company's current position.

At that point there was so much ingrained hostility to the media that the industry's capacity to think creatively about media management was crippled. Yet that was the time such thinking was needed most.

As we saw in Chapter 2, there are situations like Arthur Andersen's where even the best-laid plans prove useless—and the tobacco industry was not favored with the best-laid plans in any event. It may be that, as with Andersen, the press simply wasn't willing to listen. That being the case, it might be argued that the only course was to batten down the hatches and rely on litigation, while assuming a defensive posture on the PR front. Not promote powerful spokespersons like Donahue. Not mandate a more open-door policy. Instead, hire PR flacks to give reporters the runaround.

> *"Reporters felt compelled to play up the contents of every document,"* says Dan Donahue, senior vice-president and deputy general counsel at the R.J. Reynolds Tobacco Company. *"...If they didn't, they'd be dropped from the plaintiffs' [media] list" and miss out on something later on that might be really important.*

Yet the experience of the tobacco industry at its darkest moment may well suggest that such timidity and cynicism about the media was unjustified and unwise. It may also suggest that the industry's message points do, in fact, resonate with a significant segment of the American population.

And, it may suggest that the tobacco industry always had the option to be as proactive and aggressive as its adversaries and that, had it been proactive and aggressive, the results might have been pleasantly surprising if not downright startling.

Success, Briefly

In the late 1990s, as the state attorneys general mounted their campaign, some of the tobacco companies seemed to rise to the occasion.

Public opinion was primed against the industry at that point. Not only had respected public officials at the local level replaced plaintiffs' attorneys as the adversary *du jour*, but one of the most popular politicians in the country, Senator John McCain, put his name on legislation that, while it didn't pass, reinforced the momentum of the state AGs.

By this time, the tobacco companies had abandoned

any pretense that cigarettes are harmless. Now they armed themselves with the powerful message points about the limits of governmental power on the one hand, and individual consumer choice on the other. Shrewdly, they sought opportunities to make their case in public.

As the manager of media affairs at the Philip Morris Companies (now Altria) during that period, Dave Quast was right in the middle of that long-overdue initiative. He was on radio nearly every day debating nearly everybody. He patiently fielded call-in questions like, "How can you go home and look your children in the eye?"

During these appearances, Quast focused on his themes of individual choice and the inherent rights of his, or any, industry. But he also talked about the quit-smoking programs that the industry was sponsoring, and he did it so persuasively that, on one occasion, a representative of the American Cancer Society offered to stay in contact and possibly joint-venture a health initiative.

"We were finally taking our case to the people," says Quast.

Quast is convinced that such outreach had a salutary effect. He saw it in the Letters to the Editor columns, and it was palpable in the feedback from industry focus groups. In turn, there was a meaningful shift among the major media, or at least a helpful softening.

For example, in late 1998, when Philip Morris introduced a smokeless cigarette, there was a feature report on page 1 of *The New York Times* that Quast describes as a veritable "commercial." Just one year earlier, had Philip Morris introduced a proven no-cost cure for cancer or recipe for universal peace, the major dailies would have suspected a trick of some sort.

The smokeless cigarette had the additional value of confirming the industry's strongest message point—that, as an industry, it is selling products that are directly responsive to consumer choice. If they choose a product that is not unhealthy, the industry will manufacture it and rejoice in so doing.

To this day, "the tobacco industry doesn't know what a good job it did during that period," says Quast. If it did know, it forgot quickly. By late 1999, the proactive energies

Diluting the Story

It may or may not too late, but the tobacco industry is well advised to emphasize that its product is legal, and that adult consumers have the right to choose. The essence of a good story is two or three strong, sound ideas. From a PR standpoint, it's therefore essential to not dilute the story with ineffective side messages.

As of this writing, visits to industry Web sites highlight two additional PR initiatives that, as innocent as they seem, might well be diluting the message. One is corporate giving. All corporations give away money, but Philip Morris (now Altria) has been vociferating about its philanthropies and support for the arts. There's food for Somalia, and for the elderly. There are Old Masters on view in Houston, thanks to Philip Morris.

Many of these charities were instituted in the mid-1990s at the height of the tobacco wars, and the corporate motive therefore looks suspicious. In fact, Philip Morris may really be calling attention to alleged corporate culpability when it devotes one-half of its home page to spotlighting the company's munificence. If the message is, "we are selling a legal product, and we deserve a fair shake," you dilute that message by looking as if you're trying to buy a little love.

The shame is that the company is probably munificent under any circumstance. But it should be giving away its money quietly. Let people, especially reporters, discover the good deeds on their own.

As of this writing, the other half of the Philip Morris home page includes a link that is of little value at best and, at worst, might further enflame negative perceptions. It is a press release about its recent court victory in Oakland.

Usually, a court victory is a no-brainer. If you've got it, flaunt it! Yet the peculiar dynamics of the tobacco wars suggest otherwise. If defeats are bad, victories can be even worse from a PR perspective. Public opinion about the tobacco industry has festered so badly for so long that news of a victory in court could actually make people angrier, especially as the perception is that the industry can buy its wins outright.

"It's an O.J. scenario," agrees Dave Quast, former manager of media affairs at Philip Morris. "The guilty get off because they can afford to buy the best lawyers."

By contrast, the public does not reflexively accuse Microsoft of buying a win against the government in its epochal antitrust case, since there was no presumption of guilt, or even a widespread understanding of the issues at stake.

The irony is that once the public thinks you're guilty, any later court victories are discounted as illegitimate.

had begun to subside and industry spokespersons were once again no-commenting in newspapers throughout the world.

"It may be that, once the industry saw it could settle most cases and survive, it became too careful again," suggests Quast. It has "settled back" into the same defensive posture that served it poorly for so many years.

If Quast's surmise is correct, the tobacco companies may be assuming that settlements are inevitably perceived as admissions of guilt and that, the more they're in the media, the more damage they will suffer as a result of those admissions.

> "It may be that, once the industry saw it could settle most cases and survive, it became too careful again," says Dave Quast, former manager of media affairs for Philip Morris. It has "settled back" into the same defensive posture that served it poorly for so many years.

Thereby hangs another tale of corporate myopia. Defendants settle big cases every day without admitting guilt. In fact, it's Legal Public Relations 101. Most reporters are sophisticated enough to understand the high cost of litigation, and they know that corporations will not contest many meritless cases against them.

It's just one more message the tobacco industry should be sending, but is not.

So Don't Forget...

There are widely applicably lessons to be learned from the many
mistakes that the tobacco industry has made over the years.
In particular...

- Don't defend the indefensible. The alcohol industry
  acknowledges the dangers of its product. Acknowledge any
  dangers of yours. One insupportable position undermines all
  the credible messages that you need to get across.

- Speak from conviction. Impassioned spokespersons, with a
  clear commitment to principle, offer a human alternative.
  Reporters may not agree with you, but they'll respect you.
  And it will show in their coverage.

- Control, but don't be control freaks. By guarding your
  spokespersons too closely, you communicate arrogance.
  You may also look like you're hiding something. Don't
  manage media communications as if you distrust the media,
  even though you may have ample cause to be distrustful.

- Be proactive. The longer you stay in a defensive position,
  the more opportunity your adversaries have to find and
  exploit your vulnerabilities. If you actually believe you're right,
  look for opportunities to say so.

8

Special Agendas...
Gearing Press Relations to
Specific Practice Areas

Thus far we've looked at policies and procedures that affect media relations in the corridors of corporate power. We've also looked at some very peculiar media dynamics that have driven certain highly sensitive and controversial industries.

Every legal specialty, however, entails some special media considerations of its own, irrespective of the client industries involved.

When attorneys market themselves as "industry legal teams," with track records serving gun manufacturers or car companies or tobacco, they need to gear their thinking about the media to those industry situations. But attorneys also market themselves as antitrust experts or bankruptcy practitioners or securities litigators. Media relations play out uniquely for each specific practice area.

It is beyond our scope to look at the media issues peculiar to every legal practice area. However, by reviewing a few areas, we can get a sense of how lawyers with different substantive skill sets must do their own thinking about media, which is sometimes very different from what colleagues in other practice areas must think about.

We need look no further than antitrust, bankruptcy, and securities litigation for telling hints as to how and why media management should be tailored to accommodate disparate problems.

Antitrust: It's All About Media

There is no legal practice group more directly affected by media coverage or with a greater obligation to understand and fine-tune media relations than antitrust. It's a fact that might at first blush seem grossly overstated, if not completely incongruous, particularly since many newspaper readers don't even know what antitrust is.

But think it through.

Antitrust law is soft. Different administrations

interpret it differently. During the Nixon Administration, corporate kingpins felt the all-probing sting of antitrust law. During the Reagan Administration, antitrust law barely existed.

Even with product liability, there are limits to the impact of media. According to the law, a company is found liable or not found liable, often by conscientious juries whose personal sympathies may not be reflected in their decisions. By contrast, antitrust regulators are freer to act in direct response to what they perceive—subjectively— as corporate good citizenship, as well as to what they perceive as "best interests of the consumer."

That means, more than other regulators, the folks at DOJ or FTC or at state agencies will bald-facedly form their opinions and determine their official actions on the basis of what they read in the newspapers or see on television. They're allowed to!

Not just regulators, but the senators who write letters to the agencies are directly affected by a corporation's reputation as formed by the media. Observers point to companies like Computer Associates whose "aggressive" reputations among reporters make life more complicated every time they target a new acquisition.

The attorneys representing companies under scrutiny frequently become spokespersons for their clients and, as Mark Ostrau suggests, their credibility inside the regulatory agency is directly affected as a result. Lawyers with credibility have more leeway in negotiations. Lawyers without credibility are often limited to playing adversarial roles with the regulators.

Ostrau, an antitrust partner at Fenwick & West in Silicon Valley, points out that prosecutorial discretion is directly affected by public opinion and media track records. "Gun jumping" is a case in point, explains Ostrau. Acquirer companies often want to involve themselves in the management or the decision-making at targeted acquisitions before the government has completely finished approving the deal. Doing so can be a clear Hart-Scott-Rodino violation, but whether or not the government will act in such cases is always unclear.

Public reputation is a decisive factor.

Bad PR in antitrust matters can be disastrous. Everybody is a potential plaintiff, as Ostrau points out. Local AGs read the national press and, if they see a case going badly for a company, the news can inspire state action. The AGs, as political animals, are monitoring local popular sentiment as well, so a large company cannot afford to high-hand newspapers in Des Moines or Tacoma.

Media savvy is thus something that antitrust lawyers owe their clients, not as an addendum to their legal practice, but as a definitive component of that legal practice. Ostrau articulates the essential best practices:

- Understand that there are multiple audiences, all of them important. The consumer feeds the politician who feeds the regulator. Make sure your message points fly at the grass-roots level.

- Focus all message points on consumer interest, which is the heart and soul of antitrust decision-making. Why does your position mean better products and services at lower cost?

- Tell stories! The best way to prove that your position is in the best interest of the consumer is with narrative examples that show what will happen as a result of, say, a proposed merger. Then, let the reader connect the dots. "When this car company buys that paint company, it will save millions by using its own product for body work. That means savings for customers and returns for shareholders."

One effective approach, applicable to many business cases but particularly to antitrust litigation, is to show that it is the government—not the company—that is roiling the waters, attempting to challenge, if not altogether transform, normal and acceptable business behavior. "Where the government is trying to establish a novel legal proposition, one can certainly say the case is built on an untried theory," says James Eiszner, who heads up the antitrust practice at Shook, Hardy & Bacon in Kansas City, Missouri. "If, as in the Microsoft case, there is good evidence that the government's case will 'stifle innovation,' then that is a smart thing to say as well."

The Mother of All Antitrust Cases

You will recall that press coverage of the government's antitrust case against Microsoft was constant, protracted and in-depth, or at least more in-depth than for any other antitrust case since Teddy Roosevelt went after J.P. Morgan.

Anything less than an amiable and cooperative public posture in an antitrust case is, as a general rule, totally ill advised. Public truculence only makes the regulators more aggressive and the judges more hostile. Yet general rules can be subject to stark reversal when it comes to media strategy.

During much of the case, observers like Mark Ostrau, an antitrust partner at Fenwick & West, tended to believe that Microsoft's press strategy was as perilously obdurate as the business strategy that landed the behemoth in hot water in the first place. They saw nothing but negatives in the company's frequently bumptious refusals to comment or, when it did deign to comment, in its self-serving renditions of breaking case developments.

In retrospect, Ostrau isn't so sure. "Microsoft stayed on message all the time," he says. Their position, like it or not, had the virtue of consistency. True, they almost forced Congress to act by digging in so deeply. Yet, adds Ostrau, as risky as the strategy was, it showed a critical awareness of multiple potential plaintiffs. They were not going to give an inch, apparently because the company and its lawyers understood that, were they to do so, causes of action could spring up like weeds throughout the country.

Sullivan & Cromwell, the New York legal giant representing Microsoft, also has a history of stonewalling the press, and the firm never has paid much of a price for doing so. Their inveterate media "strategy" wasn't broken, so neither the client nor its lawyers were going to try and fix it.

According to Ostrau, an alternative strategy would have been to say to the world, "'Here's an acceptable solution to the problem. We were too aggressive. We will not engage in further exclusive dealing.'" That too might have worked, says Ostrau, had the company mounted a PR campaign to "steer opinion" in favor of the partial solution.

And—the essence of all antitrust PR—such an alternative campaign would have had to hit hard on consumer interest, underscoring the fact that a breakup would produce inferior technology at higher cost. Even amid such monumental litigation, antitrust PR is really just a glorified commercial.

"Here's our idea. Here's why it's the best deal for consumers." Period!

Such an argument puts the burden of proof on the government to show why, in an area like antitrust where customer satisfaction is the ultimate tribunal, upsetting corporate applecarts is in anybody's interest (other than the regulators who must tinker with markets in order to justify their jobs).

There is a most peculiar variable affecting the antitrust media market. As we've seen, as antitrust law is subject to vagueness and subjectivity, lawyers who comment on cases are often doing so on the basis, not of what a particular law says, but of what they think is the critical consumer-oriented issue.

If regulators can be swayed by public opinion, lawyers commenting in the press are swayed by client interests. Gary Reback, formerly a partner at Wilson, Sonsini, Goodrich & Rosati, has been aggressively attacking Microsoft for years. In fact, he represents Microsoft's chief competitors and doesn't mind admitting it.

> *A reporter once asked Fenwick & West partner Mark Ostrau, who was commenting on the Microsoft case, if he represented any Microsoft competitors. "I'm a lawyer in Silicon Valley," Ostrau responded. "Who do you think I represent?"*

Likewise, a reporter once asked Ostrau, while he was commenting on the Microsoft case, if he represented any Microsoft competitors. "I'm a lawyer in Silicon Valley," Ostrau responded. "Who do you think I represent?"

"I think the good reporters treat us like the regulators treat us when we're giving them our opinions," says Ostrau. "They look for the kernels of truth, and treat the rest of it with a grain of salt."

Bankruptcy: Bad News Early and Often

Regardless of whether they're representing creditors or debtors, bankruptcy attorneys face unique media problems. First, they have to define some angle of interest to the press regarding cases that are often purely procedural. Second, to make the story media-genic, they have to identify good guys and bad guys when often the only guys involved are broke guys.

"Creditors don't approach full victory," says Bill

Rochelle, a partner in the New York office of Fulbright & Jaworski. "So it's difficult to come up with a story."

One lawyer who came up with many such stories was Harvey Miller, a longtime favorite of reporters covering bankruptcy matters. Formerly a partner at Weil, Gotshal & Manges, Miller marketed himself as the nation's pre-eminent bankruptcy lawyer (which was probably true), thereby becoming the go-to source on any bankruptcy issue that could possibly interest the media and the public. Miller fashioned a mystique of sorts for himself, based on a rather distinctive personality style, while exploiting media interest in workouts for high-profile clients such as Macy's.

The salient media problem for bankruptcy attorneys is that bankruptcy is mainly bad news. The press loves bad news—the proverbial "Plane Lands Safely" won't sell newspapers—and attorneys and their creditor clients enmeshed in the negative coverage don't usually benefit as a result. They may even be the messengers blamed for the message or tarred by it.

On the debtors' side, "the PR is God-awful," says Rochelle. "One press release after another says the situation is 'terribly difficult' or predicts a 'great signal victory ahead.' No one can ever be quite sure what 'great signal victory' they're talking about."

Interestingly, however, media opportunities have opened up for bankruptcy attorneys in the wake of the 2002 corporate scandals. John Lee, a partner at Andrews & Kurth in Houston, points out that debtor representation can be parlayed into favorable press coverage if the attorneys makes a case, not just for the client, but for innocent people affected by the bankruptcy.

"Judges read that kind of coverage," says Lee.

Importantly, such message points directly address the primary challenge facing bankruptcy attorneys, which is to make themselves and their clients sympathetic to a public that's just as likely to panic in the face of financial collapse as acknowledge the quality of the professionals working to minimize the damage.

Bill Rochelle points toward a fundamental media strategy for bankruptcy attorneys, particularly when they're representing companies in bankruptcy or teetering on the edge. "Get out the bad news early and keep repeating it. Bad news becomes old news."

It's a counterintuitive strategy in many ways, but one that directly addresses the peculiar nature of bankruptcy practice. Rochelle, comparing United Airlines to American Airlines, notes that "UAL has crawled under a rock. They don't communicate unless a reporter traps one of their people inside a courtroom."

As of this writing, UAL has not been releasing full information or addressing specific negative questions, so the public expects the worst and that expectation keeps festering. By contrast, American has prepared the press for the worst and so the press is now inured to it. Better than that, says Rochelle, American's strategy has reversed the news cycle. The company, with all its honest acknowledgement of adversity, has made a hopefully incipient recovery the really hot anticipated story.

For companies like American Airlines, Rochelle advises one more best practice: Manage all internal communications as if they were press communiques. Companies in trouble must assume that any email or voice mail, not to mention memoranda, will be forwarded directly to a reporter.

Securities Litigation: Upping the Ante

If you are a securities litigator, the art of media relations is the same for you as for any other kind of attorney, only more so. Indeed, if there is a peculiar circumstance distinguishing crisis management for practitioners in this area, it's the mind-boggling consequences of media coverage. In this area of the law, underscore every one of our media lessons, and every one of our best media practices, many times over.

Michael J. Missal, a partner in the Washington, D.C., office of Kirkpatrick & Lockhart, offers a scenario he's seen repeated in case after case. The regulators take a very aggressive approach to an enforcement action and investors, reacting in part to the press coverage, panic. They sell. The matter is resolved and the market goes up. The investors have locked in their losses.

In one case, Missal says the sell-off was $2 billion. And there's a class action suit lurking behind every

Soup to Nuts: Media as a Bankruptcy Case Strategy

The recent corporate scandals ending in bankruptcy have made the practice area palpably more colorful and the stakes tangibly higher. The attorneys are therefore finding a more avid, responsive press.

John Lee, a partner at Andrews & Kurth in Houston, offers a telling example of how to exploit that interest. Lee launched a fervid media campaign on behalf of Vlasic Foods International, a bankrupt company spun off by the Campbell Soup Company. Campbell's alleged motive was to unload a problem business and transfer as many of its debts to Vlasic as it could get away with by manipulating the financial results and projections of the subsidiary business.

Lee sent out a press release in August 2002, fortunate timing, as it coincided with the Enron scandal. His media strategy would directly support his litigation strategy, exponentially increasing the pressure on Campbell, and on the auditors, so that, even should the case be appealed, a powerful climate of opinion would have been created.

Here was a bankruptcy case with real good guys and bad guys. In the wake of the 2002 corporate scandals, Lee was able to quadruple the impact of the press coverage on all directly interested audiences.

Lee also broke a fundamental media rule, but shrewdly so. Brevity is usually the best practice, and that certainly applies to press releases. Journalists often don't read press releases at all, and your best chance at getting their attention is with a few short newsworthy paragraphs. But Lee signed off on a very long release that marshaled evidence against Campbell as if it were the complaint itself.

"We wrestled with the press release," says Lee. "We knew we had to be careful, because [Campbell] would have loved to sue us for saying the wrong thing. But, with so much evidence, we decided the best approach was to communicate the enormity of the case, and that the best way to do that was by laying it all out."

Result: In the aftermath of the press release, Vlasic's side was sympathetically reported on Reuters and by *The Wall Street Journal*. Best of all, National Public Radio did a primetime segment that featured music—a singing group chirping,

Mmm mmm bad, mmm mmm bad
That's what Campbell's soups are
Mmm mmm bad

PR professionals have a term for that kind of coverage. It's called a "home run."

unfavorable published word, not just in *The Wall Street Journal*, but on some obscure online information service as well. In securities litigation, there's a plaintiffs' bar second to none in rapacity and for expert *sub rosa* media manipulation.

In such an environment, there's no substitute for proactive media outreach. Securities litigators must broaden and deepen their relationships with the reporters in the field. Equally crucial is to anticipate a worst-case scenario in every situation and, as Missal strongly advises, take steps to educate the relevant reporters as to the actual facts of your case.

Another characteristic distinguishing this practice area is that the cases are not only enormously high-stakes, but enormously complex as well. Left to their own devices, even seasoned business reporters are liable to get it all wrong. The solution is to assume that, in the best interests of your client, reporters need to be educated—and educated without making them feel they're the village idiots.

> "Get out the bad news early and keep repeating it," advises Bill Rochelle, a partner in the New York office of Fulbright & Jaworski. "Bad news becomes old news." It's a counterintuitive strategy in many ways, but one that directly addresses the peculiar nature of bankruptcy practice.

In a down market, proactive solutions are especially imperative, as the whole world is looking for scapegoats. Work the press aggressively, Missal advises. For example:

- Follow up on all allegations. Advise reporters when the allegations are less harsh than they might seem in statements issued by the regulators. Your goal is to always convince the press that there's no real story here, or much less of one than might appear at first glance.

- When reporters get it wrong, don't recriminate, but do point out their errors. It will mean a better chance next time—and there will always be a next time—to educate the writers or vet what they're going to publish before they publish it.

- Always be available as a free source of information to reporters, with no concern over whether or not they're going to cite you as an expert in their articles. You maintain enormous credibility by unselfishly helping out on matters where you're disinterested.

From Mole Hill to Media Mountain

When Turner Communications hired Michael Milken as a consultant in the mid-1990s, you'd have thought from the coverage in newspapers throughout the United States that it was the biggest story since he and Boesky were convicted in the first place.

Milken, of course, was barred from trading in securities. He was still on probation when Ted Turner enlisted him. The intense press coverage, which clearly pointed toward a blatant violation of the ban, kicked off an investigation by both the DOJ and SEC.

In fact, Milken was not trading in securities. He was merely acting as a consultant. As a source close to the situation now reflects, Turner's response was a classic case of helpless reaction to the media when a methodically proactive approach was needed.

Effective early media outreach would have ideally relied on a simple analogy to deflect the story. Analogize Milken to anyone who acts as a liaison and collects a finder's fee for his efforts. The intricacies of securities law would have been boiled down to just such basics, leaving little room to charge Milken with dealing or Turner with complicity.

The reinforcing point would then have been to tell reporters what Milken would have actually needed to do to break the law. Thus do you box in the reporters by anticipating their skepticism. By describing what a violation would look like, you reassure them that they're not missing something in the situation that's incriminatory. You've covered all ends of the imbroglio without recourse to a single legal arcanum.

Yes, the regulators would have read the results in the press and acted accordingly. And, a story on page 5 instead of page 1, even were it to still question the propriety of the engagement, would have been far less likely to catalyze official action.

A proactive media approach is all the more critical to balance the constant feed of information from the other side once lawsuits start getting filed. In particular, Milberg Weiss Bershad Hynes & Lerach, until its recent split-up the nation's largest securities plaintiffs' firm, was a veritable media machine.

As Missal points out, some plaintiffs' firms often put the media in touch with seemingly "pathetic" victims of the alleged securities scam. Those pathetic victims may finally turn out to be diversified investors worth seven figures. It's always helpful to steer reporters to the truth if doing so discredits your opponents or opens reporters' eyes as to who is really manipulating them.

So Don't Forget...

Since dynamics differ from one type of crisis to another, individual legal practice groups face unique challenges when dealing with the media. For example,

- Antitrust practice is media-driven. Antitrust law itself is all about subjective judgment. Anything that gets printed can affect how regulators, politicians and their constituents regard your client—and can decisively tip the scales on prosecutorial judgment calls.

- Bankruptcy is bad news. The press loves bad news. Your task is to find the social benefit and underscore it in human terms—the retiree whose nest egg is being salvaged, for example. And get the bad news out and keep it out. That way, when there is good news, it's the angle that reporters may likely turn to and focus on.

- Securities litigation translates into billions of dollars. But the law is complex and most reporters get it wrong. Be proactive, be patient, and always look to minimize the import of every enforcement action.

9

Another Crucial Complication…
How Cultural Differences Affect
Media Management Across Borders

Martin Beirne delivers a rather chilling assessment of how differences in media cultures from nation to nation can affect the coverage of crises internationally.

Beirne, a founding partner of Houston's Beirne, Maynard & Parsons, was representing a Rome-based order of the Catholic Church during the awful scandals of 2002. He was awakened by a call from the Vatican, informing him that reporters and camera crews were suddenly descending on the Order requesting interviews. The journalists included a contingent from American television.

"You wouldn't think there would be that much of a problem, since Italians are so used to dealing with aggressive paparazzi," sometimes on a 24/7 basis. But, added Beirne, that ignores an essential differentiating fact. As Italians, "paparazzi assume that they have immortal souls," and that they need to pay some attention to how their behavior may affect the disposition of those souls post-mortem.

Not all journalists from other nations necessarily acknowledge such constraint.

Beirne's is a worst-case scenario, to be sure, in terms of cross-border media relations. The prospects aren't always so grim, however. In March 2003, Bayer faced its first trial in defense of the anticholesterol drug Baycol. Throughout the trial, plaintiff's lawyer Mikal Watts took every opportunity to remind the jury that Bayer is a foreign (German) company.

Under the circumstances, Watts had good reason to wield a xenophobic cudgel. The trial was occurring in Corpus Christi, Texas, a reputedly "plaintiff-friendly" haven and a region known for strong protectionist sensibilities. Yet the tactic failed. It failed, in part, because Bayer Aspirin has been, for decades, too much a constant of American consumer life to arouse any dread of economic infiltration. But the tactic also failed because the jurors were perhaps too intelligent to rise to the bait. There had been no anti-German screeds in the Texas press, nor might the jury have been affected if there were.

There are innumerable gradations on the cross-border spectrum. Lawyers, for example, will find that a partner defection from one law firm to another, or some other typical industry event, could inspire glaring tabloid-like headlines and speculation in the UK legal press. In the United States, *American Lawyer* or *The National Law Journal* might yawn off the same event.

In any event, no discussion of media relations in a global legal marketplace is complete without a look at how attorneys can make crucial adjustments to indigenous media cultures and, in so doing, achieve better results for clients facing crises or lawsuits abroad.

Let's consider what happens to potentially unpopular foreign clients under scrutiny in the United States.

Finding Common Agendas

U.S. media outlets are usually too sophisticated to want or need to attack non-American litigants in the United States. Even if a foreign company has been blithely ignoring SEC regulations, the readers of *The Wall Street Journal* won't necessarily be any more outraged by the reported malfeasance than by the activities of Mr. Skilling or Ms. Stewart. Those readers do business with foreigners every day.

Yet even purportedly fair newspapers like *The New York Times* or *The Washington Post* may sometimes find that your client's nationality is an issue—and sometimes legitimately so. The lawsuit or crisis at hand may be relevant to current trade policy, for example. Or, the situation has resulted in such strong public opprobrium related to national or political factors that the public reaction itself is newsworthy.

Then there are the countless other media outlets that directly reflect, and often cater to, their readers' national or regional fears. When BP Petroleum pulled out of Cleveland, Ohio, a few years back, and thousands of jobs were lost, the local media was much more hostile than if it had been Exxon Mobil. When President Chirac does not go to war in Iraq, your French client may have a tough time winning a lawsuit in Cheyenne, Wyoming.

And, if subtly anti-foreign pressure is being exerted against your client by the President of the United States, then, as Thomas Wilner discovered, you've got a real media problem. Wilner, a partner in the Washington, D.C., office of Shearman & Sterling, found a surprisingly inquiring press in the mid-1990s when he was representing Mexican vegetable growers in a trade dispute with Florida.

At issue were Mexican exports competing with Florida tomatoes. Normally, The Tomato War might have been relegated to the back of the business section, except in the *Miami Herald* and other Florida publications. But the timing was not propitious. President Clinton was up for reelection and dead set on carrying Florida. The Presidential team went to the press.

In such situations, Wilner will usually take two immediate steps. "The first thing I do is list all my messages," he says. These are the substantive points that stand the best chance of getting heard on the client's behalf. "The next thing I do is list all the possible messengers," including client representatives, experts, supportive third parties and himself. (Often, Wilner advises, the attorneys in his cases are the spokespersons actually preferred by reporters.)

> "The first thing I do is list all my messages," says Thomas Wilner, a partner at Shearman & Sterling. "The next thing I do is list all the possible messengers," including client representatives, experts, supportive third parties and himself.

Since such situations entail a battle over public opinion, and involve public perceptions of foreign interests, the messages are seldom strictly about points of law. They are social and political.

As social and political messages, they must in some way overcome or defuse the implicit chauvinism of the opposition, or the opposition's powerful (and often legitimate) focus on local jobs and local interests. When we look at Wilner's campaigns over the years on behalf of foreign clients in the United States, we find a shrewd pattern of changing the agenda. In other words, he pursues a different but equally relevant political discussion in which reporters and the public are likelier to be on his side.

The tomato fracas is a case in point. Wilner went to the press with alternatives to the "Mexican Tomato Growers Are Snatching Revenue from American Tomato Growers" message. In particular:

- Florida's tomatoes are "gas green," meaning treated with chemical substances. Mexican tomatoes are red right off the vine. They're better for the environment. They're better for your health.

- These red right-off-the-vine tomatoes are available to Americans only from Mexico. Most Americans, including Floridians, prefer the Mexican tomatoes. The opposition is interfering with free market choice.

- The tomato growers in Mexico are very, very poor. The tomato growers in Florida are very, very rich. They have also been charged with polluting the Everglades.

Any one of these message points might not have sufficed to overcome Florida's impulse to protect Floridian interests. No single argument might have defused instinctive media antipathy to foreign interests. But taken together, they formed a broadly sympathetic political platform that won the media war. When a Clinton lieutenant talked with *The Chicago Tribune*, the paper put him on the defensive and wouldn't let him move past the issue.

The case settled on terms mutually favorable to Mexico and Florida, and Clinton carried Florida anyway. "It was one of my greatest accomplishments," teases Wilner.

Here, it was the message points themselves that decisively changed a specific political landscape in favor of a foreign party. In a more recent fight with another U.S. President, it was the use of the right spokespersons that leveled the playing field.

When George W. Bush introduced steel tariffs, Wilner's overriding goal on behalf of his client Arcelor, a Belgian/French/Spanish steel company, was to show that tariffs are bad for the U.S. economy. An immediate goal was at least to win key exclusions for as many of the client's products as possible.

One Winnable Fight...and One Much Tougher

It's challenging enough to prevail in the media on behalf of a foreign client when powerful political interests line up against you. It's profoundly more difficult when the foreign interests have been vilified from the outset.

Thomas Wilner, a partner in the Washington, D.C., office of Shearman & Sterling, represents the Organization of Petroleum Exporting Countries (OPEC) in antitrust cases in the District of Columbia and a federal court in Alabama.

From a media standpoint, there are two problems. One is the residual hostility some media sources and the public harbor against OPEC, dating back to the oil crisis of the 1970s. The other is that the suits were filed by David Boies, a master of media relations.

Wilner prevailed in both lawsuits—they're currently on appeal—in part because he developed pointed messages that anticipated and defused anti-OPEC sentiment. Wilner advised a low media profile and did not seek to litigate the cases in public. But he readied himself for media inquiries—not with legal arguments—with politically sensitive points designed to put OPEC itself in proper context.

- OPEC nations are poor. For most, oil is their one natural resource. For Nigeria, it's 80 percent of the economy,

- It's economic imperialism to apply our laws to how other countries handle their own resources in the global market.

- The United States behaves no differently with its own resources in some cases. For example, the embargo on Cuba guarantees the United States an OPEC-like stranglehold on sugar.

- Americans buy gas-guzzling vehicles. When we do that, we exacerbate the problem.

Such messages had a decisive effect, Coverage by the Associated Press and *The New York Times* has been supportive.

In another matter, Wilner faces a much rougher road.

As of this writing, the U.S. government has been detaining Kuwaiti nationals at Guantanamo Naval Base. Wilner believes it's an illegal detention and is representing a dozen families in an effort to secure release.

During the Iraqi war, the media was unresponsive. Reporters demurred, waiting for a changing news cycle to encourage a less hawkish editorial tone.

With the media, timing is everything, although that's no doubt cold comfort for the detainees.

Wilner commissioned an economic study that supported the general anti-tariff message, which was well received by the press, since the economist who worked on it was an articulate messenger. Support from the National Retail Association was likewise salutary.

But the real victory for the client may have occurred more at the local level, because the spokespersons were local residents who told how badly they'd be hurt by having to pay more for specific products that Arcelor was providing.

The message reversed the protectionist impact—to protect Americans, we must liberalize foreign imports. But the message was also significantly enhanced because the case that was made to the media was not argued theoretically by lawyers or economists, but by average American citizens.

The politicians may have listened to a message about the macro effects of tariffs on the economy delivered by an expert spokesperson. But they really heard the message about local consequences delivered by local people in local media. Result: More Arcelor products were excluded from the tariffs than those of any other affected foreign steel concern.

Target Europe

If the Battle of Waterloo was won on the proverbial playing fields of Eton, a fight just across the Channel waged by Arco Chemical before the European Commission over a site license, was won in the editorial columns of the *Financial Times*.

For companies doing business on foreign soil, one critical media objective is to secure broad political support. It is indeed a political struggle, all about changing the agenda and replacing one ideological hot button with another. We've looked at how such cases play out in the United States. They may well play out the same way in any nation. Only the specific hot buttons vary from country to country.

A very different issue in cross-border media management is the use of media to directly affect decision-makers. Here, the media strategy must sometimes be very finely tuned, because we're not just taking aim at an amorphous creature called public opinion. We can't just plaster the Sunday

Supplements and hope for the best. We must learn instead about each media market, about what the decision-makers actually read and about how substantive discussions must be packaged for maximum impact.

Media target marketing is especially well-advised in Europe. According to Ian Forrester, a partner in the Brussels office of White & Case, European decision-makers are circumspect about what they read and which publications they allow to affect their decisions.

For antitrust lawyers in Europe, "decision-makers" most often means the European Commission, while the European courts are not so susceptible to direct media influence as courts in the United States. There are no jury pools to influence, and thus no reason for corporations to curry public favor in order to win, say, a product liability case. Non-European companies should certainly worry about how the European press characterizes them— their reputations, their products, their services—for all the obvious marketing reasons. But there isn't usually a direct connection between public opinion and case outcome.

> "Vox populi *is not an issue for the courts,"* says Ian Forrester, a partner in the Brussels office of White & Case. "But I am in no doubt that the European Commission is sensitive to how things appear to the public and in the media" on all specific issues related to their policy-making function.

"*Vox populi* is not an issue for the courts," says Forrester. "But I am in no doubt that the European Commission is sensitive to how things appear to the public and in the media" on all specific issues related to their policy-making function.

The question is: Which public? Which media?

As we saw in Chapter 8, American antitrust lawyers can reach decision-makers through any number of media venues, even including local dailies in smaller cities. In the United States, a shotgun approach over time can be a very effective ongoing weapon for or against, say, Microsoft. In Europe, a company that has a lot riding on EC policy decisions ought to be hiring lawyers and media advisors who know precisely which media to play and when. Otherwise the message never gets through.

That Arco case, handled by Forrester, is illustrative.

Arco, facing the prohibition of single-plant limits on site licensing of technology, took its argument to the EC. But as Forrester interpreted the Commission's leanings during the early stages of the case, his client's position was likely to be rejected. It was at that point, with less to lose, that he helped arrange for the *Financial Times* to run a debate on the subject.

The debate was neither tendentious nor one-sided. All points of view were covered in what Forrester describes as a lively and informed discussion. Yet Forrester says he is now "quite confident" the *Financial Times* feature turned the tide in favor of Arco as the comments there by informed supporters of the company's position provided crucial additional public endorsement.

The point, though, is that it was the *Financial Times*, not *The Times of London*. "They [the EC] don't read *The New York Times* [either]. They might see *The Wall Street Journal Online*," says Forrester, but they don't read the newspaper with any regularity.

According to Forrester, the Commissioners do read *Le Monde*, *Frankfurter Allegemeine Zeitung*, and *Neue Zürcher Zeitung*—a major Swiss newspaper, with an international readership—as well as the *Financial Times*.

Depending on the kind of case, Forrester might also call specialty writers at the *European Voice*, a Brussels- and London-based weekly launched by the publishers of *The Economist* in 1995 to cover EC regulatory and political developments. He might also call various writers at Agence Europe in Brussels, which puts out a number of publications monitoring the EC, including an important update called *Europe Daily Bulletin*.

In Europe, clients expect their attorneys to call the press in order to affect EC decisions, especially when things seem to be going badly, as in Forrester's Arco matter. The art of the press interview itself does not vary as radically from country to country as one might expect. The nuances of personal communications change according to culture, of course, but there are abiding professional similarities among journalists. Some of the same best practices apply everywhere.

For example, Forrester is careful with all reporters to emphasize during an interview when he is on the record and when he is not. "I will craft my on-the-record quotes while I am talking to the reporter, and I will ask to check the quotes before the article is published." Reporters worldwide normally honor this request.

Especially for complex business matters, there is a universal need to simplify. Journalists in France are as bemused by legalese as journalists in New York, and the same sound bites that get the job done for you and your client in one country will do so in another as well—no matter how sophisticated the outlet.

So Don't Forget...

Cross-border media relations is about protecting clients in potentially hostile environments. It's all about politics.

- Change the message. Foreigner-as-enemy is just one message. Craft alternative messages that shift the debate and appeal to popular public agendas that serve the client's interests.

- Enlist third-party support. The right spokespersons will identify your foreign client as being in the same camp as local interests. It's no longer us-against-them when some of "us" have the same goals.

Cross-border media relations is about figuring out how to reach the right people on foreign turf.

- Pick your targets. In Europe, the regulators are highly susceptible to media influence—but there are just a handful of publications where you can exert that influence.

- Follow the same rules. Brevity is everywhere the soul of wit and all readers respond best to sound bites. Journalists in most countries that have a free press play the same game— they've all got deadlines, and they all know the difference between on and off the record.

10

Law Firms in Trouble:
Unique Media Strategies for a
Unique Market

L et's take a look at a few less than pleasant realities confronting law firms in the 21st century.

First, there have always been crooked attorneys and incompetent attorneys, and they were just as fair game for reporters in 1903 as in 2003. However, with the growth of civil litigation in our lifetime, law firms themselves have also become targets simply because, for plaintiffs' attorneys, that's where the money is. If an attorney has merely said hello to Skilling or Fastow during the last few years, his or her entire firm may now be named in some class action somewhere.

Second, it's not just plaintiffs' firms fishing in deep pockets. In the 1990s, one law firm after another fell victim to the FDIC and its Office of Thrift Supervision as the government sued just about everyone who ever represented S&L kingpin Charles Keating or other failed thrift operators throughout the country. Many thousands of average citizens had lost their money and the political pressure to punish all involved parties was intense.

New York's Kaye, Scholer, Fierman, Hays & Handler was the worst-hit law firm. The firm argued that its representation of Keating was zealous advocacy, not only permitted but mandated under the professional canons. It would have cost a fortune to prove it, however, so the firm finally settled, although not before it was featured several times on the front page of *The New York Times* as well as in other major newspapers.

Government interest in allegedly errant law firms continues. Right now Enron-involved law firms are DOJ and SEC targets, not just plaintiffs' targets in civil litigation. In the current environment, lawyer-client confidentiality is under siege and any erosion of that sacred principle means only more personal liability for lawyers and their firms.

Third, the *American Lawyer* publishes law firms' per-partner profits every year. That editorial feature has changed the complexion of the American legal profession more profoundly than any other single development in its history. It means that everyone can peek into your business and draw whatever conclusions they want as to your competitive viability. Worse, it has made for exponentially greater numbers of partner defections as attorneys shift from reportedly less profitable firms to others reportedly more profitable.

Ideally, a partner departure will only rate a sentence or two in a local legal newspaper. The good news is that, because there are so many partner defections, it takes a little more than the event itself to make it newsworthy. The bad news is that the events often are newsworthy because the partner is so high-profile, because the departure signals stormy weather for the firm or because a whole practice group has left.

Moreover, partner defections are sometimes so acrimonious that they can generate any number of ancillary problems as well. When one well-regarded but relatively unknown attorney named Frode Jensen decided to leave Pillsbury Winthrop for Latham & Watkins, the result was a lawsuit and national scandal spiced with sex as well as money.

In the late 1980s, firms tried hard to punish defecting partners by denying portions of their receivables based on non-compete clauses in partnership agreements. A banner case was the suit filed by New York's now-defunct Lord, Day & Lord against a tax partner who left the firm and took a major client, *The New York Times*, with him. Lord, Day did not prevail.

It was an ill-advised effort in any event, as it ultimately drew negative press attention to Lord, Day. It's just unseemly for attorneys to sue each other. The legal press loves it, but clients don't. "Law firms really ought to settle these things as fast as they can," says Leslie Corwin, a partner in the New York office of Greenberg Traurig, who points out that restrictive covenants are just not enforceable in the legal industry.

Corwin should know. He has represented both partners and firms on both sides of diverse partnership disputes. Most famously, in the 1980s, he represented Evan Dawson, a partner dismissed by White & Case.

Finally, there is an overriding consideration that makes media relations during any law firm crisis uniquely less tractable than with other organizations. The judgment against Lord, Day was based, to a substantial degree, on the fundamental principle that, by enforcing non-compete clauses, law firms deny clients their basic right to free choice of counsel.

In a sense, that emphasis on client rights reverberates in any discussion of the options law firms have for handling public imbroglios, including what they can and cannot say to the press. Law is a thoroughly client-driven business, after all, and clients maintain not just the right to choose counsel, but to confidentiality as well.

Law firms' lives are therefore not their own. Any press strategy must be tempered by what's best for a client even when it may not be the best strategy for the firm itself.

Optimal Middle Ground

At the same time, a virtual paranoia about how clients will react to public comments by their attorneys paralyzes many firms confronted with crisis. The result is that they finally exert no control over what reporters wind up writing and what the marketplace winds up thinking.

Conversely, attorneys are also inclined to want to control messages. It's an inclination that often makes them less than ideal press sources in general. Such extreme circumspection can prove utterly crippling if the news topic at hand is a departed partner or an SEC investigation or a client representation that went seriously awry.

As media attention will predictably continue to increase, both in the legal and general press, it is therefore imperative that law firms evolve media plans and best media practices, just as their clients in the tobacco or gun industries have done under the withering scrutiny of regulators and reporters. For law firms, such planning must walk a delicate middle ground and take careful measure of client interest even as it maximizes the law firm's message about itself.

Here are Les Corwin's prescriptions for law firms, to be administered as prophylaxis before a crisis occurs and to control the damage once the bad news goes public.

Codify your policy

All organizations need to designate crisis spokespersons and, as appropriate, exclusively limit press access to that spokesperson. With law firms, the need is acute. In a flat and politically charged organization, random and contradictory statements by partners can be deadly. The flip side of law firm paralysis is law firm entropy; that is, any number of self-justifying or self-interested partners may feel no constraint about taking their personal agenda to the press or responding on their own to random press inquiries.

> *"The partnership agreement itself should contain a crisis clause that assigns exclusive authority to a single person, usually the managing partner, to speak for the firm," says Leslie Corwin, a partner in the New York office of Greenberg Traurig.*

Corwin offers a definitive solution that takes into account these unique political vagaries that can roil a law firm in crisis—put it in your partnership agreement! "The partnership agreement itself should contain a crisis clause that assigns exclusive authority to a single person, usually the managing partner, to speak for the firm," says Corwin.

The clause could also include a mechanism defining a crisis. For example, it can stipulate that any litigation involving the firm itself constitutes a crisis. Depending on the firm, it can also stipulate that any presumably negative event affecting the firm, even the defection of a single partner, triggers the crisis clause.

The idea is additionally salutary in light of attorneys' typical reverence for the written word and its binding contractual impact. In lieu of a crisis clause in the partnership agreement, managing partners typically send out memoranda to the partnership as crises occur, warning against speaking to the press and commanding every single member of the firm to direct all press inquiries to his or her office.

Such memoranda are always a good idea, but if they're not backed up by a solemn declaration in the partnership agreement, they are perceived more as tactical stopgaps than ironclad policy.

The buck stops here

As the firm spokesperson, the managing partner should be trained to deal with the press. (Formal media training is available from outside sources.) Inexplicably, law firms often choose their leaders with absolutely no regard for their ability to communicate with the outside world, either during crises or in the normal course of business. It should be as basic a job skill as the ability to read a financial statement.

The crisis clause may include an option for the managing partner to also designate additional spokespersons should the situation warrant. Corwin advises that the law firm's outside counsel is often a wise choice, particularly if the managing partner is personally at risk in a crisis or too close to a situation to maintain sufficient equilibrium.

Reporters know a rudderless ship when they see one. When the *American Lawyer* did a feature over a decade ago on Boston's ill-fated Gaston & Snow, reporter Peter Carbonari turned up at the firm and, as Corwin recalls, "said, 'take me to your leader.' He was shuffled off to [the executive director], some guy who used to work at NYNEX." (Corwin represented one of the partners during the firm's dissolution.)

It seemed as if the managing partner had totally abdicated his role as spokesperson, confirming Carbonari's impression that the firm was floundering. The impression was correct. The managing partner had, in fact, abdicated his leadership role altogether. Attorneys must run law firms and speak for them as well.

Don't let them see it first in the newspaper

There are two specific audiences that you need to immediately speak to at the first whiff of public crisis. The first is internal.

The largest corporations in the world take pains to advise their employees when a major scandal or investigation is occurring. For law firms, the need is acute. Your partners feel entitled to that information even more importunately than might high-level executives in a hierarchal corporate organization. If they feel blindsided, the negative effects on the firm, in terms of internal comity, will likely be worse and go on longer than the crisis itself.

At the same time as you are communicating internally, consider contacting every key client you believe might care one way or another about the unfolding crisis. At the very least, it's a courtesy and relationship-building gesture. At best, it defuses any real concerns clients may have about your ability to continue doing their work.

Enlist third-party support

Once you've contacted clients on the eve of crisis, it then becomes easier to solicit their public statements of support. During its S&L ordeal, Kaye, Scholer's very ability to function as a law firm was directly questioned in the press. The crisis was snowballing, just as it did when Arthur Andersen's clients began doubting the firm's capacity to continue to do business.

Kaye, Scholer's response was to choose a new chair, Michael Crames, who made it his business to settle the case as fast as possible. But the firm also directed reporters to important clients—big ones like Texaco—and friendly general counsel willing to publicly express their confidence in and commitment to the firm.

Such endorsements begin the process of converting negative messages into positive ones. The comments in the press by these in-house supporters were, if nothing more, reminders to the world that Kaye, Scholer did indeed have a blue-chip clientele.

The media tide never did turn dramatically in Kaye, Scholer's favor, but the firm was at least able to convalesce. As the settlement dust cleared, the convalescence included shrewdly placed mentions in the press of attractive new partners in growth areas such as intellectual property joining the firm. Crames remained accessible to the press throughout the period.

Many law firms would not have survived. A decade later, Kaye, Scholer remains a strong Manhattan law firm.

Take the initiative

You can be sure that a bad story about your firm will not be ignored; it will be publicly dissected. At law firms, with so many inmates running the asylum, there's seldom enough nerve to tell the story first. But it can sometimes be the best practice for major events like a government investigation (subject to advice from outside counsel) as well as less cataclysmic partner defections or branch office closings.

The advantages are threefold.

First, it takes you off the defensive. Reporters see the story differently when they see you're unafraid to discuss it.

Second, it gives you the first shot at making your point—that the investigation is without merit, or the firm is still strong despite so-and-so's departure for a competitor.

Third, it sets you apart from other law firms. Reporters are often impatient with lawyerly reticence and institutional foot-dragging. A bold, proactive disclosure helps define you as a no-nonsense organization. It suggests that you are well run and decisive.

Don't fly solo

Corwin believes that the same rule applies in PR as in litigation: Law firms that do not seek outside expertise have their own foolish selves for clients. Outside advisors not only know more about the press than you do, they're dispassionate as well. Their decisions are grounded in reason, suggests Corwin, not self-defensive emotion.

Law firms should pick outside advisors who know the legal market inside and out. There are a finite number of legal publications and you ought to expect your PR people to have personal relationships with reporters at every single one of those publications.

In the UK, those reporters bring a tabloid-like ferocity to their coverage of the legal profession. If the London market is at all important to you, expect to be poked at, jeered at and negatively depicted. You can minimize the damage via London-based PR professionals friendly with editors and reporters at every single UK legal publication.

What Do We Say?

The political tinderbox that exists normally at so many law firms makes press relations a uniquely challenging task on all levels. It certainly makes message development difficult. Partners will cavil at this angle; they'll scoff at that angle. Ultimately, the managing partner must sign off on all messages in all situations and resolutely stand by them.

A Universal Problem

One thing law firms in trouble have going for them is a legal press, which may at times be unfair but is at least fairly sophisticated, especially when it comes to marketplace trends.

Legal reporters know the problems attendant with growth. They know that, as law firms expand, it becomes increasingly difficult to maintain a seamless professional culture or to adequately monitor the behavior of all their partners.

Legal reporters will still blame firms for breakdowns, and they should. But their understanding of the market can at least temper their philippics when law firms articulate a comprehensive but succinct message to address the crisis and deliver it sympathetically.

A case in point is a global law firm that was dismayed to learn that one of its partners was stealing immense amounts of money. The attorney's practice was so abstruse, it would have been hard to detect the malfeasance under any circumstances. With the firm's attorney ranks then in excess of 700, the criminal was able to escape unnoticed for quite a while.

Good move number one: The law firm made no attempt to deny the problem or to avoid press calls.

Good move number two: The managing partner is a soft-spoken, somewhat avuncular person, with the wise but unprepossessing tone of a Walter Cronkite.

Good move number three: The firm really only had one message point, but it was powerful. *If it can happen here, it can happen anywhere.*

For seasoned legal reporters, that message was both credible and comprehensive. On the one hand, it made the story larger than the firm itself. It made their crisis a profession-wide crisis, which means the discussion of it in the press was not a down-and-dirty ferreting out of firm-specific facts. Instead, it was a discussion of a universal problem, of which this particular firm was just one example.

Finally, the message point reinforced the fundamental excellence of the firm itself by reminding reporters and their readers that the real significance of the scandal was that it would actually happen to such a wonderful organization.

One publication even ran the message point as the headline of the story.

When dealing with the general press, assume the reporters know very little about the overall dynamics of how law firms operate in the marketplace, much less the subtle nuances. It is an esoteric business, after all, so be prepared even to explain what a practice area is. If you're Kaye, Scholer in the 1990s, don't assume the reporter knows that you were supposed to zealously represent Charles Keating. Explain it, carefully and emphatically.

With the legal press, you can assume varying degrees of sophistication, but in most cases, an *American Lawyer* or *National Law Journal* reporter will know quite a bit about the marketplace. You can play such knowledge to your advantage if, for example, you are losing a partner.

Assume the departing partner is not a rainmaker. As Corwin suggests, you can hint to reporters that the departure relates, in part, to the firm's aggressive growth posture. The departing partner—while an extraordinarily talented practitioner—does not fit with the firm's "high standards" in terms of business development nor does his particular practice "fit in with the firm's goals."

Assume the departing partner is a rainmaker. Here, the firm should remember that the primary readership (aside from directly affected clients) is other attorneys. Corwin suggests an open acknowledgement that the firm will miss the departed lawyer and will be actively looking to replace him or her.

It's a free job advertisement. Most readers won't see weakness, they'll see opportunity if they're at all interested in making a change, particularly for more money, or to go a firm like your own that may have a better profits-per-partner index than their current one.

In other words, the very forces in the legal marketplace that cause law firms such public as well as internal headaches can be played to their benefit, if the firm is organized, coherent —and just a little braver than many law firms usually are.

So Don't Forget...

Law firms have media issues that virtually no other organization faces. Client interests rule, and non-compete covenants don't work. To hoe the tough row...

- Include language in your partnership agreement that designates one spokesperson, usually the managing partner, in the event of crisis—and specifically prohibits press contacts by other partners unless expressly permitted.

- Communicate immediately with all partners, apprising them of the crisis. Communicate immediately with all key clients and, if possible, enlist those clients as supportive press contacts during the crisis.

- Rely on outside media advisors, but be sure that those advisors have good personal relationships with reporters at every important legal publication in the country.

- With general media reporters, assume they know nothing of legal industry dynamics. With legal trade reporters, assume a fair amount of sophistication, and use their knowledge of the profession to support your message points.

11

'Switch the Witch:' The Immense Significance of Offense in Crisis Communications Today

Going on the offense means hitting them as hard as they hit you, or even harder.

Not just responding to accusations, corporations and individuals can challenge the credibility, the motives, even the decency of their accusers. Sometimes going on the offense means hitting them *before* they hit you. That political activist in the Northwest has long been an enemy of your industry. He's attacked other companies in the past and there's every reason to believe he will target you should a likely occasion arise. Let's see what kind of legitimate, related intelligence we can get on him now.

A media campaign based on offense would seem to be just one more item to add to the list of strategic options for attorneys and PR professionals during crises. It is that, of course—in fact, it is often the first option to consider.

Yet "offense" has a greater significance as well, directly related to many of the fundamental themes underlying public communications in our society today. As such, it is certainly an appropriate subject to conclude our book on media relations amid litigation and crisis.

Tactically, offense "introduces risk to your attackers," says Eric Dezenhall, president of Nichols Dezenhall, a crisis-management firm in Washington, D.C. At the same time, it is an effort to "inoculate" a specific audience, perhaps a jury pool, or consumer segment, with a specific message about the company or with its position on a key issue.

"Inoculate" is a precise usage here as well as a term of art. It denotes a process whereby serum is put into the public bloodstream so that future messages from the opposing camp—"germs," if you will—will be systemically rejected.

Most companies prefer the defensive. On the one hand, going on the offensive is uncomfortably reminiscent of the bad old days when corporations did go after their critics, but with altogether indefensible tactics, as when General Motors assigned a squadron of corporate goons to trail Ralph Nader and hopefully uncover compromising sexual behavior.

Yet in the larger sense defensiveness is, at least these days, "in their DNA," as Richard Berman, president of Berman and Company, a communications firm in Washington, D.C., points out. Not that companies lack resources for an offense. What is publicity if not an offensive measure, only with positive, feel-good, self-promoting messages?

But transforming the corporate publicity machine into an attack mechanism is problematic, and often impossible, for a couple of reasons. First, as we discussed in Chapter 2, converting of one type of talent (for promotion) into another (for crisis management) requires effort. Whether the crisis calls for a defensive or an offensive strategy, it will demand a particular mindset that garden-variety publicists may presently lack.

Yet there's a more basic reason why corporations remain in a defensive posture. To go on the offense often means taking not just a big risk, but also a very special kind of risk. On the one hand, capitalists take risks all the time. Risk management is part of doing business. They test new markets, invest in new products and sometimes they lose their money. In a crisis, smart capitalists often see, or can be taught to see, how the risks of not going on the offensive may clearly outweigh the risks of unleashing the Dobermans.

On the other hand, an offensive campaign can require a corporation to enter a socio-political fray where it will be taking sides, not just on specific issues, but in ongoing pitched battles between different segments of our society—plaintiffs in general versus corporate defendants in general, hawks versus doves, environmentalists versus energy producers, conservatives versus liberals, and so forth.

As Berman points out, corporations are in business to do business. They want to sell their products and make their shareholders happy. The status quo is their ideal. All this other stuff gets you onto an awfully slippery slope. No matter how they may personally feel about social issues, corporate executives are mighty uncomfortable siding with anyone in that ongoing 21st-century event known as the "culture wars."

Take a company like Coors Brewery. The great spurt in sales that Coors enjoyed occurred only after the public was lulled into forgetting the radical right-wing orientation of its founders, including opinions that had nothing to do with the labor squabbles in which the company was also involved. To maximize growth, to compete with Budweiser, you just can't limit your consumers to Goldwater Republicans.

Often, however, an industry's enemies are using or have even created a crisis specifically to score points in these culture wars. Rightly or wrongly, the products they're attacking, the corporate integrity they're questioning, are mere pretexts to propagate and reinforce their own larger agendas in the media and in the marketplace. The lawsuit against a hotel franchise we discussed in Chapter 1 was all about Muslim-American political aspirations, not the unfortunate experience of one hotel.

That being the case, a corporation may have no choice but to enter this fray. In some cases, going on the offensive guarantees that a corporation will, at some level, find itself engaged in a media-based debate on what the whole world ought to look like.

For a corporation, that is risky business to be sure. For the attorneys who help corporations respond to crises, it also means a summoning forth of all their skills and knowledge to help their clients stay on the safe side of libel. And, it means an all-the-more solid commitment on the part of attorneys to crisis planning and a guaranteed, active role for attorneys on the crisis team.

Finally, it requires of attorneys a stern measure of self-transcendence, because attorneys—at least corporate attorneys—don't much like risk of any sort. Yet here we are adventuring the riskiest edge of public relations.

Which Side Are You On?

Corporations need only scrutinize the forces perennially arrayed against them to understand why there is often no way out of the culture wars. In particular, Berman points to the Non-Government Organizations (NGOs) as "institutional enemies...They are permanent enemies. They will never go away. Their agendas will never be satisfied. Environmental groups will always hate the lumber companies.

The Naderites will always hate General Motors."

Berman has advised a variety of industries on how to deal with the NGOs and with concerted efforts by plaintiffs' counsel to target specific industries. Most recently, he has been a spokesperson for the restaurant industry in its obesity crisis.

In such litigation, the plaintiffs' bar is as agenda-driven as the NGOs. Today it's fatty fries, tomorrow, something else. But the impetus is not necessarily just money. The agenda is also iconoclastic, anti-corporate and perhaps even revolutionary.

The choices for targeted industries are to fight back and swallow the bitter pill of socio-political involvement when they'd rather just be selling products—or else surrender the field to resolute and often ruthless antagonists.

Berman cites a number of additionally persuasive justifications for an offensive attack.

- NGOs, if not plaintiffs' attorneys, always start off with a better image than the companies they're attacking. They don't seem self-interested at all. They don't care about money. Corporations obviously do. "The ultimate weapon of the NGOs is credibility," says Berman.

- NGO public-spiritedness is underscored by their names. "People for the Ethical Treatment of All Living Things" sounds a lot more trustworthy than "Anaconda."

- They are driven by passion. Historically, passion tends to overthrow the empires built by greed. Staying on defense becomes tiresome. In this mode, companies feel less in control. They often suffer from "issue fatigue."

- The battle is "asymmetrical," with the Davids on the NGO or plaintiffs' side fighting ceaseless guerilla war against corporate Goliaths. In this context, they can often self-justify illegal actions as the terrorists did on 9/11 or, more sympathetically, as the Norwegian underground did against the Nazis. Less constraint provides them with decisive tactical advantages in some situations. It's their slingshot.

"Start the offensive now, before they start attacking," counsels Berman. The incessant crises and protracted struggles that corporations endure prove that, whether they like it or not, they are seen by some as permanent socio-cultural nemeses.

But scattershot counteroffensives are not enough. In fact, Berman advises that potential enemies be identified now and carefully scrutinized on an ongoing basis.

Maybe some NGO hasn't yet launched a specific offensive against your industry, but there's every reasonable prognostication that, in the fullness of time, it will do just that. Berman advises permanent surveillance as a prophylactic response.

"If you were the president of a timber company, say, wouldn't you like to read in the newspaper that the head of some environmental NGO has just been indicted for embezzlement?" suggests Berman. There may not be anyone with the incentive to find out how an NGO's finances are being handled other than the company it's attacking.

Such ongoing surveillance by our corporate fathers may seem to have an Orwellian tinge, but Berman points out that the NGOs are tax-exempt organizations feeding at the public trough. "Excellent research" and a passion for the "truth" are legitimate corporate weapons to keep these adversaries honest.

> *"They (NGOs) are permanent enemies," says Richard Berman, president of Berman and Company, a communications firm in Washington, D.C. "They will never go away. Their agendas will never be satisfied. Environmental groups will always hate the lumber companies. The Naderites will always hate General Motors."*

Corporations should be "watchdogs," using the media as messengers for their own interests and agendas. They have as much right to do so as Ralph Nader and the social justifications for doing so are often every bit as high-minded.

Picking Your Fight

There is more art than science to media management during crises, and the decision to go on the offensive is no exception. One generally sound and rather obvious best practice is to take a hard look at your case. If it's a good case, advises Eric Dezenhall, then it's usually a good time to go on the

Anti-corporate Terrorism: A Daily Occurrence

Non-Government Organizations (NGOs) have decisive advantages in their sorties against global corporate capitalism. Passionate, agenda-driven warriors, they don't expect to win by simply arguing their cases in the media. The really radical ones know how to fight hard on many fronts. They know how to spot the soft underbelly. And they will utilize every weapon at their disposal to exploit it.

Richard Berman, the president of Berman and Company, a Washington, D.C. communications firm, cites one instance that shows just how formidable an NGO can be—and how a counter-offensive media strategy is both possible and necessary.

Huntingdon Life Sciences is a UK-based biosciences company with offices and investors throughout the United States. It does chemical testing on behalf of large companies and, since it uses animals in these tests, the company fell perilously afoul of an NGO called Stop Huntingdon Animal Cruelty (SHAC).

SHAC's tactic was to intimidate the employees, not of the company itself, but of its suppliers, actually going to people's homes and demanding that they pressure their employers to stop doing business with Huntingdon.

SHAC struck pay dirt with Marsh & McLennan, a major insurance company selling to Huntingdon. The insurer bowed to the pressure rather than invest a considerable sum in fighting back simply to support one small and, by its lights, insignificant customer.

The British government stepped in and eventually provided Huntingdon with insurance. But SHAC had sent a potent message to other NGOs: *This is how you can fight and win! This is how you should fight and win!* Meanwhile, as a parallel strategy, SHAC put so much pressure on investment firms Merrill Lynch and Charles Schwab that both companies eventually announced that they would no longer trade Huntingdon stock for investors. Other firms followed suit.

According to Berman, there should have been no alternative for Huntingdon except a media campaign to expose SHAC's methods. SHAC's methods raise serious legal issues, by the way. It was equally important, therefore, that the media campaign *make people afraid to be associated with the organization.*

It is always an option, and often a necessity, to go after your opponents as purposefully and as methodically as they are going after you.

offensive. If your adversaries are corrupt, or their position seriously mitigated by circumstance, sound the charge!

If it's a weak case, the better practice may be to develop your message points and then hunker down in the trenches. On the other hand, there are numerous instances when corporations or individuals will go on the offensive because it's simply the only thing they can do. By contrast, candid, defensive disclosures in response to negative coverage may create further legal exposure and possibly criminal or civil actions.

Apologies are often ineffective. Some common wisdom these days holds that Martha Stewart should have immediately apologized for what she allegedly did. Dezenhall questions that wisdom. "Had Martha Stewart apologized, she would have been indicted in a nanosecond," he argues.

Apologies are likewise ineffective when the charges against you involve a chronic pattern of malfeasance. "You can't apologize for twenty years in five minutes," advises Dezenhall.

People in such situations are cornered. But, if they may have no choice except attack, what should they actually tell the press?

The crucial criterion for your message—which can be delivered either on the record or *sub rosa*—is that it be related to the issue at hand. Personal dirt is useless and sex will "backfire," says Dezenhall.

The important exception is when such personal behavior is, in fact, relevant to the charges flying back and forth. For example, conservatives preaching family values are fair game for exposure if they're cheating on their wives, says Dezenhall, a former media advisor in the Reagan White House.

The decision to launch a first attack, before the press gets hold of the story, also hinges on the case itself. Often, the purpose of the "inoculation" isn't so much to attack the adversary, but to prepare the media with message points that you know you'll need to use once the battle has begun—so why not use them now?

Dezenhall, for example, cites work he did on behalf of the pharmaceutical industry in a case where people committed suicide after using a particular psychotropic drug. It was easy to see where the attack lines would eventually be drawn. Before any attack was launched, medical experts assertively reminded the media that these were very sick people from the get-go.

Because the press heard that message without asking

for it, it was all the more credible. Because it was offered
proactively, it sounded like something the company *wanted*
to say rather than something they *had* to say.

Make the Messenger the Message

Often the message points that guide an offensive strategy
are totally amenable to the corporate client. Dezenhall's
pharmaceutical client had done nothing wrong, after all.
Its message was effective in any event and had the added
advantage of being true.

Life, though, is not always quite so simple. In many
instances, not only must the company choose sides in a war
it would rather not fight, it must communicate in a way
that is not always straightforward. As Dezenhall observes,
so much PR is an attempt
at a rational explanation
of how the company has
done something right or
why it has not done some-
thing wrong.

> Apologies are ineffective when
> the charges against you involve
> a chronic pattern of malfea-
> sance. *"You can't apologize for
> twenty years in five minutes,"*
> advises Eric Dezenhall,
> president of Nichols Dezenhall,
> a crisis-management firm in
> Washington, D.C.

But the dynamics of
crisis communications are
not necessarily rational. In
fact, the key component in offensive campaigns often
involves "fogging the issue" (a term of art among the folks
who do it for a living).

Fogging the issue means changing the story. To do so
you need to find an alternative—and legitimate—story that
the press will jump at. In a classic offensive strategy, that
alternative story is about the accuser: how the story is being
developed, how and why information is being planted, how
the media is being played. The media doesn't like being
played, and they will aggressively turn against an accuser if
they feel they have been manipulated.

As an example, Dezenhall was brought in a few years
ago by the feminine-hygiene industry to defend against
Internet-generated attacks on its products (which were all
the more newsworthy because they could revivify the toxic-
shock syndrome cases of a decade earlier). Working with
investigative reporters in major media, he helped trace the
sources of the attacks to an "all-natural" feminine-care

product manufacturer self-interestedly targeting a larger marketshare. News stories exposing the source of the cyber rumors began appearing, and the public and the consumer media became more cautious about the health "tips" they were getting from anonymous Internet sources.

One of two things could have happened at that point: The all-natural tampon manufacturer would become the focus of negative media interest or, as was the eventual outcome, the story would simply go away. In fact, that was the ideal outcome, as Dezenhall's client was finally insulated from any negative media interest in its industry.

It is thus worth noting that the purpose of an offense may not necessarily be to harm or defame the adversary. The real purpose may be to attack them enough to simply bury their story.

In any event, the name of the game is "Switch the Witch," as Dezenhall calls it in his novel, *Jackie Disaster*. It is especially effective for guilty clients or compromised clients. The purpose of an offensive strategy in this context is to find a worse villain. By doing so, you change the subject of the story altogether.

Sometimes the media itself becomes the story if it has covered a case in a slanted way. It's a delicate media relations strategy, but the press does sometimes delight in self-laceration as a way to show how conscientious and thoughtful they are about their role in society. Your bad story doesn't go away altogether, but it could become the secondary story.

The company can emerge as a sympathetic victim of media sloppiness or hysteria. Its products or executives may even be conspicuously exonerated as a result of such media *mea culpas*.

To some extent, Martha Stewart might have been able to "switch the witch" by questioning the media's coverage of her case. "Rather than an apology, an option could have been for her to hammer home just how much overkill was going on in the press," suggests Dezenhall. Of course, there may never have really been a media solution available to Martha Stewart at any point, but making the press self-conscious about its own preoccupation was at least a tactical shot worth taking.

Fogging Issues, Clarifying Values

"Corporations need to invest in the culture wars," says Eric Dezenhall, president of Nichols Dezenhall, a communications firm in Washington, D.C.

Indeed, they may have no choice if their adversaries throw down the cultural gauntlet. In some situations, an investment in the culture wars will simply win big lawsuits.

The public's core values engender sympathy for the opposition in many cases. The goal then may be to befog the issue, and one way to do that is by focusing on the plaintiffs' attorneys themselves. "People don't actually hate trial attorneys but at some level they think they should," quips Dezenhall. One offensive tactic is to therefore deflect public attention from the case by spotlighting the role of attorneys who make millions telling the world what to think.

In other cases, the public instinct may seem to be in your favor. The goal of an offensive campaign in these situations is to "give people permission to embrace their own values," as Dezenhall puts it. For example, there is enough palpable public contempt for the plaintiffs' position in the obesity cases to support an effective attack campaign by the restaurant industry.

The subsequent standard media pitch (and legal argument) is that consumers have a choice of product, and that they are not compelled to buy what the restaurants are selling. Dezenhall calls this the "PR 101" message.

Alas, there's not enough staying power in that message, says Dezenhall. It's been used elsewhere, notably in the tobacco wars. There, the "core public values" were whittled down anyway, with disastrous results for the defendants. An expanded PR message in the obesity fracas must therefore include "sedentary lifestyles" or "bad parenting" or other such themes to attune the public's ear to a broader view of the plaintiff's case.

The obesity cases may turn out to be a particularly telling example of the need for an offensive strategy. As of this writing, we are already beginning to see the public's "core values" get "whittled down" or at least challenged, according to Richard Berman, the president of Berman and Company, a communications firm in Washington, D.C., who represents the restaurant industry.

"*The New York Times* is already expressing sympathy for plaintiffs and broadcast journalists are already leading with questions like, 'Obesity—Who's Responsible?' as if there were actual doubt about it. The other side will always sell their story if you let them."

In response, Berman ran a national TV spot spoofing trial attorneys who are suing a Girl Scout for selling cookies "that taste good on purpose." He has also gone on the offensive with attack print ads in major news magazines. All the TV networks have covered the campaign, thus underscoring the original message. In fact, says Berman, "we've gotten more 'earned media' [i.e., independent coverage as a news story] than what we've paid for."

Many of the purported media crisis coups of recent years were really just celebrations of shrewd PR strategies—in other words, stories about the story. According to Dezenhall, there was nothing particularly remarkable about how Johnson & Johnson handled the Tylenol crisis. Everything they did was pretty standard procedure, including the recall, and, with a ready-made external villain (the psychopath tampering with their product), there was no question of corporate culpability at any point.

It was a no-brainer.

Yet, in collaboration with their PR advisor, Burson-Marsteller, Johnson & Johnson created a story, in fact, a legend, all about their own public-spirited responsiveness.

There was no attack or offensive campaign here. None was necessary. But the dynamic is instructively similar. You find an alternative story that will outlast and outshine the one you'd prefer to bury. Sometimes the alternative story is all about the accuser. Sometimes it's all about the messenger.

As long as it's not all about you!

So Don't Forget...

For corporations, going on the offensive is risky and repugnant.
But your adversaries have dragged you into the fray whether you
want to be there or not. So as long as you're there...

• Identify your inevitable enemies. Often these are NGOs
  that have resolved to wage a permanent war against your
  industry. Go after them first. Expose their methods if those
  methods are reprehensible. Target their funding sources.

• Deliver your messages before you're asked. You know
  the sorts of defensive points you'll need to make if you're
  sued or attacked in the press. If you make those points
  now, before the fight has started, the media might very
  well believe them.

• Deflect unfavorable stories. By attacking your attackers,
  you create an alternative villain. By questioning the coverage
  itself, you may even make the media—not yourself—the
  centerpiece of media coverage.

• Make your attacks relevant to the issue. Sexual or other
  personal revelations will usually backfire. On the other hand,
  if they're calling you greedy, use any evidence you have
  of financial improprieties on their part, and use it for all
  it's worth.

CONCLUSION...SORT OF

*The study of media relations during crises
and during litigation can neither be
conclusive nor comprehensive.*

If real conclusiveness were possible, crises wouldn't be
crises. They'd merely be situations that periodically arise
and are successfully addressed by pressing a few
time-tested buttons. Clearly, though, media management
is part art and part science. When art is involved, there
are always things left unsaid.

We've often advised in these pages that the best of
best practices should, in certain instances, be jettisoned.
Yes, "no comment" is almost always a bad practice,
for example. But "almost" is the operative word. There
are times when you and your client should simply hide.

Comprehensiveness is equally impossible in the
art of media management. Right now, Corporate America
is suffering a protracted crisis that exploded first at
Enron. This particular crisis has affected and, to one
extent or another, changed how crisis managers understand
their jobs. Next year, or the year after that, a new and
equally critical, but very different, cultural event may
loom large for attorneys and their diverse clients. It may
require new rules, new approaches and new best practices,
or at least a rethinking of current practices.

Crisis means having to adapt to radical, unforeseen
environmental changes. Mr. Darwin knew his stuff!

Even absent some sea change on the socio-political
front, we cannot be comprehensive in our discussion.
Many industries, like the tobacco industry or the
automobile industry, face crises that are peculiar to their
markets, and that require crisis managers to tailor very
specific solutions. Addressing them all is well beyond
our scope.

Let's conclude then, not with a final word, but
with an invitation. Perhaps your industry grapples with
unique media issues affected by fact patterns or marketplace variables that require separate treatment. Let us
know. Let's explore those idiosyncratic exigencies.

You'll be a welcome contributor to our next edition.

Appendix A

A Law Firm Crisis Management Primer for In-house Counsel

Crisis and media management represents not just an ancillary service provided by law firms, but a critical component of case strategy in litigation practice. Crisis management is a two-way street, a partnership between inside and outside counsel to which law firms, drawing on diverse client representations, can sometimes apply invaluable battle-tested experience.

A few years ago, Michael Wagner, a partner and litigator at Baker & McKenzie in Chicago, as well as a former journalist, prepared a primer for clients that neatly sums up, and adds to, many of the best practices enumerated in this book. Recently, Wagner updated the outline for a General Counsel symposium that his firm hosted earlier in 2003. The guidelines are presented in unabridged form.

***Minimizing Legal Risk While Managing the Corporate Crisis:
A Primer with Proactive Strategies and Practical Suggestions***
Copyright 2003 Michael J. Wagner

I. The Importance of Preparing a Crisis Management Plan and Assembling the Team

  A. *Why Are Proactive Plans Necessary?*
    1. The legal risks and financial stakes are simply too high.
    2. Corporations can no longer afford to be reactive rather than proactive.
      a. If your company is aware of a problem and fails to address it, it could face the specter of punitive damages in many states.
      b. Remember those who failed—and learn from their experience.

  B. *Members of the Team*
    1. Senior management
      a. CEO preferred
      b. CFO also should be involved, both for financial and for securities disclosure implications.
      c. General Counsel—the team's quarterback
      d. Key vice presidents
        (i) Human Resources—to ensure appropriate, accurate information flow to your employees
        (ii) Sales and Marketing—to gauge customers' response and keep them in the information loop at a critical time
        (iii) Risk Management—to deal with insurers and address potential liability concerns with General Counsel and outside counsel

2. Outside counsel
   a. Agile SWAT team approach
      (i) interviewing witnesses
      (ii) retaining consultants
      (iii) preserving work product and attorney-client privileges
      (iv) interacting with regulatory authorities (e.g., state, local and federal public health agencies, EPA, OSHA, USDA, FDA)
   b. Absolutely essential where litigation is anticipated or inevitable
3. First-rate public relations counsel
4. Risk manager—May be in-house or outside firm

II. Reducing Liability Risk and Damages Exposure: Implementing the Plan and Mobilizing the Team

A. *Speak With One Corporate Voice*
   1. Remember the Six Cs:
      a. Concerned
      b. Clear
      c. Consistent
      d. Credible
      e. Concise
      f. Compassionate, especially in the case of a catastrophe
   2. The importance of consistency cannot be overestimated
      a. Closing the loop of communication is critical.
      b. Inconsistent comments by company employees and middle managers in different locations can create major liability problems—especially in areas such as quality assurance, corporate compliance and risk management ("We maintain the highest standards" versus "Sometimes things fall through the cracks") and government regulatory compliance ("We adhere closely to government standards" versus "We do the best we can, but sometimes the red tape is too much to bear ...").
   3. Clarity enhances credibility
   4. "No comment" is no help—and often hurts
      a. Presumption of guilt: Survey data shows consumers/public believe companies that do not comment are guilty, hiding something, or otherwise responsible.
      b. A missed opportunity to earn trust with key stakeholders: Customers, shareholders, public, media (both general and financial), regulators, lenders and creditors

B. *Have the Team—and Especially Outside Counsel—"On Call"*
   1. General counsel or other designated corporate liaison in charge of disaster planning is the "hub of the wheel," coordinating communications to ensure a consistent prompt response and minimize liability exposure.

2. Home, office and cell phone numbers of all team members, especially chief outside counsel, should be on your Blackberry, your speed-dial, your Contacts directory, your Rolodex and at your fingertips.

C. *Once the Crisis Hits, Outside Counsel and the Designated Corporate Liaison Should Mobilize and Meet As Soon As Possible*
   1. Interviewing key witnesses and/or participants to ascertain what happened—and how to keep it from happening again
   2. Working with—and reassuring—the appropriate regulatory authorities
   3. Retaining consultants and industry experts can help companies chart the correct course early—to get at the root of the perceived problem or media target area, to reassure regulatory authorities, and to suggest appropriate proactive strategic responses (e.g., revamp or reaffirm GMP and product safety protocols, evaluate food preparation policies, reassess corporate compliance programs).
      a. Government or former government officials should be involved wherever possible.
         (i) wrapping the company in the mantle of regulatory credibility
         (ii) avoid the "shill syndrome"
   4. Multi-jurisdictional crises require multi-jurisdictional responses.
      a. For problems that arise in more than one forum, an outside counsel firm with a national or, better yet, international presence and substantial resources, is often in the best position to respond in each venue, if necessary.
   5. Protecting and preserving legal privileges
      a. Attorney-client work product privileges may vary widely from state to state, so familiarizing yourself with the scope of protections afforded in the state(s) at issue is essential.
      b. Witness statements or consultant findings that fall within a broad blanket work product protection in some states, or in federal court, may be automatically discoverable in other jurisdictions.
      c. Beware of PR privilege pitfalls: Though the recent case law trend is encouraging, no bright line test or road map has emerged yet

D. *Don't Get Hoisted on Your Own Petard: Avoiding the Careless Email and Paper Trails*
   1. Especially important when dealing with groups presenting potentially high litigation risks (e.g., sales representatives, R&D, Quality Assurance)
   2. Educating staff through internal training.
      a. Counsel should advise employees that what they say in writing could follow them around long after they leave the company or even retire.
      b. A healthy perspective: How would this look in litigation?

3. Explore whether any renegade or disgruntled employees are playing a role in the problem.
    a. Let staff know that a "boys will be boys" mentality will not be tolerated.
4. Evaluate whether the local or regional manager is well-respected by the rank-and-file—to ensure that reliable information is getting to the top.
5. Ensure that the key decision-makers have direct contact with those in the center of the storm.

E. *Ambush Prevention Strategies*
    1. To avoid liability problems and ensure a consistent response, place "friendly reminder" emails and faxes near key points of contact with the media or other constituency.
        a. Locations: Phone, cashier, receptionist, local manager's office
        b. Advise staff who the designated corporate voice is.
        c. Let those located in the likely line of media contact know what to do when the media onslaught comes.
    2. Rapid communication is the key, since every plant, facility, store, outlet or restaurant becomes a potential target even if only one of them is facing a crisis.

F. *If You Are Planning to Take Statements, Conduct Tests, or Make Findings, If At All Possible, Do Not Reduce Them to Writing Until You Have Good Reason to Believe the Results Will Be Favorable or Supportive.*
    1. Especially important in litigation-prone areas
    2. Why create unfavorable evidence for your opponent's closing argument to the jury? ("Don't take my word for it. The defendant generated it.")
    3. Exception: Some regulatory requirements and agencies may limit your options and leave you little choice.

III. **The Absolute Importance Of Becoming A Non-Story— And Getting Off The Nightly News**

A. *Remember There are Two Courts About Which to be Concerned— The Court of Public Opinion and the Court of Law.*

B. *The Longer Your Crisis Attracts Media Attention, the More Likely Inconsistent Statements—And Potential Liability Problems—Will Arise.*

C. *If Liability Looks Likely (and Even in Some Cases Where It Does Not but Your Losses in the Court Of Public Opinion Look Sufficiently Daunting), Do Your Best to Settle Soon, Settle Quietly, and Settle Confidentially.*
    1. Verify that the state where the problem arose will permit confidentiality agreements.

2. Even in those states less likely to enforce confidentiality agreements, seek to obtain confidentiality anyway.
3. Advise management and/or the appointed "point person" about the importance of avoiding admissions in conversations with claimants and potential plaintiffs.
4. Customize settlement releases for the precise complaint or series of complaints; bring your laptop to the site to tailor the document quickly, according to the exigencies of the particular situation.
5. Preparing the media release and public statement
   a. Above all else, demonstrate concern.
   b. Correctly framing the issue is critical.
   c. Describe what steps your company has already taken— and what steps it plans to take—to resolve the crisis.
   d. Work closely with other team members, especially in-house/outside counsel and public relations consultant, in crafting the final draft.

D. *Beware of Winning the Liability Battle, Only To Lose the Sales War*

Appendix B

Scenarios

Media crisis management related to litigation is an area of such increasing interest that, in 2003, the first professional conferences for lawyers (not just PR and communications professionals) were held on the subject in the United States. New York-based NorthStar Conferences was a pioneer, sponsoring programs in New York and San Francisco. Additional conferences are now being organized in Los Angeles, Chicago and London.

Litigators from law firms and their in-house corporate counterparts from all parts of the country are attending these events. The large turnout and keen interest among lawyers is a sure sign that our insistent point in these pages—that crisis teams must draw on the best legal as well as PR counsel, and that these teams must plan ahead and plan together—is being heard loud and clear.

Among the popular features at these conferences are role-playing sessions in which participants from both the faculty and audience practice their media skills for message development and delivery. Such role-plays are fictional scenarios that suggest a number of the themes we've touched on and point toward many of the best practices we've advised.

Below we've included a number of these scenarios. They are practical tools for readers to reflect on how they'd react in such exigent situations. Hopefully, your PR and legal teams can make direct use of the scenarios for role-playing and training exercises, whatever the nature of your business or the particular kind of crisis you may someday encounter.

Any similarity of these scenarios to actual events is purely coincidental.

I. Product Liability: Reassuring the Public, Protecting an Investment

You are the in-house general counsel of The Tick-Tock Watch Company. The company has just brought out an illumination product called EverGlo that is the first of its kind in the market. Simply touch the watch and the watch face glows. EverGlo was launched just in time for Christmas, 2003. It is projected to represent 20 percent of Tick-Tock's total global revenue in 2004, and likely more in the coming years.

Last week, Tick-Tock's environmental compliance officer informed the general counsel that a routine check of the company's Peoria headquarters, where the watches are manufactured, revealed an abnormal concentration of CS-511, a low-level toxin. A residue of CS-511 was used in an industrial cleaning solvent by Tick-Tock three decades ago.

As the low levels of toxin were found on the edge of the Tick-Tock property—a sprawling suburban landscape of a few hundred acres—the toxin may not be present as a result of Tick-Tock's use. The neighboring community has been there as long as the Tick-Tock headquarters, and CS-511 had been commonly found in some household cleaning products years ago.

Both the U.S. Environmental Protection Agency and the Illinois EPA have been notified, with the state agency taking the lead in the investigation. The regulators are not interested in divulging information to the press, and they appreciate Tick-Tock's assiduous self-reporting of the matter. Unfortunately, the press has picked up the rumors anyway.

The press is also well aware of how, 60 years ago, radium had been used in the manufacture of watch dials, which allowed them to be read in the dark. As a result of the radium, a number of Tick-Tock's employees (mainly female) developed tongue cancer from licking the brushes to make the tips fine enough for painting dials. It became an industry-wide problem, but, as one of the largest watch dial manufacturers in the United States, Tick-Tock is the company remembered for it.

A few minutes ago, Tick-Tock's in-house press officer, who only handles product public relations, informed you that the local daily newspaper called for a statement. It was the lead business reporter who usually gets his stories on the front page of the paper. Worse, his stories, when they include national angles, are occasionally picked up by the wire services and run in major dailies around the country.

If the story goes on for too many days, calls are likely to come in from other major newspapers in the state, as Tick-Tock is one of the largest employers in the Peoria region.

Local coverage is likely to be fair, but nonetheless critical. The more negative, the more likely the story will get picked up by other papers. Restricting the story to local coverage would be considered a victory, since it would then be less likely to have much, if any, impact on Tick-Tock.

No prepared statement is ready. The Peoria reporter is expecting a call back from a Tick-Tock spokesperson within three hours. As GC, you call your outside counsel. After a discussion of the legal issues, you ask for media advice.

- Does the company return the reporter's call?
- If so, who should the spokesperson be?
- What should the focus of the conversation be?
- Are there any ground rules you want to set?
- Should you prepare a statement?
- What should the statement say?
- Do you acknowledge responsibility?
- What should your overall media strategy be?
- What questions should you ask?

Once you have answered these questions, prepare for the actual live interview.

II. Reputation or Litigation: Weighing Opposing Risks

The CEO wants to see you in 15 minutes about a legal matter that may be in *The Wall Street Journal* tomorrow. You, the chief legal officer of Hartwell Department Stores—a publicly traded retail giant with 1,000 stores in North America—walk into a large conference room to find the CEO with a tense look in his eyes. Beside him sits the public relations director and the heads of marketing and product lines, all with nervous expressions on their faces.

The CEO reminds everyone that, not too long ago, the company entered into an exclusive agreement with Benicia, an upscale design company, to supply goods. Everyone at Hartwell considered the deal a great coup and expected increased sales from the arrangement. A multi-million dollar contract was signed, the initial shipments of the goods were delivered, and, indeed, Hartwell happily watched its sales dramatically increase.

This deal was only the latest in a series of shrewd moves by Hartwell involving Benicia. Just five years ago, Hartwell was a largely blue-collar-based business. As Hartwell picked up Benicia lines, it successfully changed its image to reach middle-class and upscale customers as well. The recent agreement on exclusive distributorship caps this strategy.

Hartwell's customer base now cuts across class lines. The alliance with Benicia is an important business relationship, to be sure.

But in the past several weeks, Benicia has received negative press over a number of its ads that are offensive to Hartwell's essentially conservative core customer base. Some of the ads are overtly sexual. Others are insensitive to handicapped people. By association, the public outcry has spilled over to Hartwell. The head of PR tried to disassociate the company from the bad press by issuing press releases, but, so far, the effort has failed.

Hartwell had warned Benicia about the ads before the bad press began. In fact, there's a paper trail, including letters to Benicia from Hartwell executives, as well as memoranda summarizing meetings in which those warnings were repeated.

The CEO looks around the table. "Any ideas what to do?" he asks.

There's no easy answer: If you terminate the contract, you'll violate the agreement and open up the company to a lawsuit. But if you honor the contract, the company's reputation will continue to be attacked. Meanwhile, sales of Benicia products by Hartwell have dropped 40% since the bad press began.

Essentially, the task is to evaluate two different types of risk.

Is there a middle ground that the company can find where it can quell the public disapproval and still honor its contract?

If so, what is the message? How is the message to be delivered?

If not, which alternative risk is worth taking? What is the worst-case scenario in taking the reputational risk? What are the advantages in doing so?

What is the worst-case scenario in taking the legal risk? What are the advantages in doing so?

What information does the company need, and what information do you need, to render an informed judgment?

Can the letters and memoranda expressing Hartwell's past concerns about the ads be used now to help Hartwell, either legally or in the press?

How fast can a decision be made? Fast enough for tomorrow's *Wall Street Journal?* If not, is there a "holding statement" you can issue that will satisfy the reporter for now, without undermining the further statement you will make once a decision is made?

The CEO needs to leave this meeting armed with both a general strategic plan as to what kind of risk Hartwell will run, as well as specific action points to implement the strategy.

III. The Cross-Border Factor: Corporate Crisis Amid Political Crisis

The Paris-based LeFlore Corp. has just suffered major economic reversals in two of its most important divisions: in-flight food services (the Regale division) and a large food import/export division (the Appetite division). LeFlore must reduce force worldwide and may even close the Regale division altogether, as it has never really recovered from 9/11.

Hardest hit are 500 Regale employees on both U.S. coasts, as well as 100 Appetite employees in California. Around 100 employees in Europe are also facing termination: these European positions are scattered throughout various LeFlore divisions.

On May 1, LeFlore announces that the first round of layoffs will begin on July 1 in both the United States and Europe. There is no accompanying statement as to the economic condition of the company, nor any reference to the future viability of any particular division.

On May 10, the California city where Regale has its U.S. headquarters files suit, claiming breach of promise. LeFlore had made a 10-year commitment to the city when it first negotiated its U.S. site, although the language of that written commitment is fairly vague. The following day, three women in an upstate New York town where Appetite has a service division file separate suits, each claiming sexual harassment by a supervisor (who is American).

As senior U.S. in-house counsel for LeFlore, you have been advised by Paris to take charge of the litigation. You are well aware of the economic realities (including the possibility that Regale might have to dissolve), and you are also aware that anti-French sentiment has been percolating because of the Iraqi war.

Calls from local reporters in California and upstate New York have poured into the corporate press office—most of them just after the layoff announcement and before the filings of the lawsuits in New York. None of the calls were answered. There is no additional statement beyond the original announcement. And no message points are prepared. You're working with an empty slate.

Now comes a worst-case scenario: the head of LeFlore's communications department advises that *The New York Times* has picked up the story. While the *Times* reporter may himself be above French-bashing, the fact that LeFlore's announcement has caused intense community response on both coasts is newsworthy. Anti-French hostility is the subject and LeFlore the poster boy.

The *Times* reporter wants an interview now (Wednesday) for the Friday edition. He will likely ask you to comment on the anti-French feelings. He will also ask about the company's situation and why the layoffs are necessary. He may or may not ask about the merits of the lawsuits. There is a strong likelihood that more newspapers in major markets will subsequently cover the story as well, including the tabloids.

There are any number of vital points that must be covered with your legal and PR advisors:

- Should you talk to the *Times* reporter? Should you now talk to any or all of the local newspapers that called?
- Should you be the spokesperson, or should an outside advisor talk to the press?
- What comment if any about U.S.-French relations would serve the company's interests? What kind of public statements might insulate LeFlore from the political situation?
- What kind of public statements might defuse local tensions?
- Can you, or should you, disclose just how dire Regale's situation is and that it might close altogether if drastic steps aren't taken?
- To what extent can you address the specifics of the suits by the city in California and by the female employees in upstate New York?
- Can you comment on the disproportionate number of layoffs in the United States?

While you're on the phone with your outside legal and PR advisors, your communications director chats with the *Times* reporter and wins a delay until next morning. You've no choice but to do the interview, but you do have a little more breathing room to prepare.

IV. Media Terror: Protecting Reputation During a National Panic

In 2001, the Al-Jeddah Bank, based in Saudi Arabia, earmarked $6 billion in equity for diverse U.S. investment. By 2005, it will have taken strong positions in major urban real estate developments, with a half-dozen separate limited partnerships coast to coast. The bank is working closely with a number of Americans.

One month later, Al-Qaeda attacks New York and Washington. One year later, flamboyant plaintiff's counsel Todd Morris sues more than a dozen Middle Eastern financial institutions, including Al-Jeddah, for allegedly funneling money to terrorists.

A blanket denial has already been issued but there have been no personal responses to media inquiries in either the United States or the United Kingdom. No strategy has been developed since the suit was filed.

A major network investigative reporter has contacted the bank's office in Paris, where Al-Jeddah's president has been conferring with his advisor. In a brief message, the reporter informed the bank that Morris claims to have decisive evidence of a sizable wire transfer.

Morris fashions himself a social crusader and is probably not interested in a settlement. Any defeat for Al-Jeddah in court may mean literally thousands of derivative suits. Any negative press coverage can torpedo its U.S. projects. It is essential to send messages that will reassure the bank's American partners, at least enough to keep them from bolting the various projects.

Total potential exposure is clearly in the billions.

Al-Jeddah's president wants to know what else he can do besides maintaining innocence in the U.S. and U.K. media. And, he wants to know what surprises might be in store from the media.

V. Health Care: Sending the Right Message

Last week a class-action suit was filed against Bankable Health Provision, a large national HMO, for refusal to reimburse Viagra prescriptions over a stipulated cost threshold. In making the decision, the company was taking a calculated risk. As CEO, you are fully aware that there are contractual issues that will likely engender high-volume litigation. That liability was weighed against the skyrocketing costs of Viagra. The decision was made to go forward with the reimbursement limits.

Working with an outside PR firm, a strong "message point" was developed that maintains the HMO's right to set arbitrary but reasonable limits and makes the additional argument that a prescription for any drug, in the face of untenable volume, is subject to such limits by all insurers.

Enough Viagra reimbursement cases have been dismissed in recent months to reassure Bankable Health that the litigation risks and exposures are acceptable.

This morning, however, a bombshell exploded. Bankable Health Senior VP Louis Lipp talked out of school to the *Chicago Tribune*. He is quoted as saying: (1) Too many people are using Viagra recreationally, not just as a treatment for impotence; (2) Too many doctors are prescribing Viagra without sufficient medical cause; (3) A drug like Viagra will bankrupt the health insurance industry; and (4) We shouldn't be paying out claims just so people can have sex every night.

The headline in the paper is "HMO Giant on Viagra Counterattack." Pfizer, the manufacturer, refused to comment for the story. But one Big Pharma spokesperson is quoted, depicting Bankable Health's position as "unsustainable," while further suggesting "there are a number of health insurers in this country who are probably in the wrong business."

You'll deal with Mr. Lipp later. Right now you have to deal with two newswires and four other national newspapers ready and able to portray Bankable Health as a company that takes an antagonistic view toward Viagra in general, and, judging from Mr. Lipp, one that opposes rather personal views of whether such a drug should even be prescribed.

Your PR advisor and general counsel hurry to your office. The task is to determine:

- What damage has Lipp's comments done both to your litigation/business strategy and to your reputation?
- Should you proactively launch a media campaign to clarify the company's position or hope the story dies down before the depositions begin?
- What do you say to the press right now?
- Do you still pursue your strategy to limit reimbursements?
- Do you change your central message point?
- Should you disassociate yourself from Lipp? If so, when and how?
- Do you call Pfizer for any reason?

More is at risk than just the class-action suit that's already been filed. Copycat litigation is an obvious possibility. Defeat in the media and in the courts can mean lasting damage to the company's reputation while you wind up paying the claims anyway.

VI. Big Pharma: Disadvantaging the Handicapped

MartinJackson Inc. has aggressively cut shipments of its arthritis drug Vigorate to Canada, since thousands of Americans are paying 30 to 50 percent less by ordering the drug on the Internet. Two related developments spell trouble. First, the leading senior citizen advocacy groups have denounced MaritinJackson's move in the press and are promising formal retaliation in the form of protests and boycotts.

Second, a leading competitor has proactively informed the world that it will not decrease shipments of its arthritis drug to Canada because, according to a press release, "we do not choose to interfere with the rights of arthritis patients, young and old, to find the best prescription drug solutions for themselves."

MartinJackson has also just launched a multi-million dollar TV campaign to market Vigorate, guaranteeing that the negative story will be refreshed in people's minds whenever they see the commercials.

A full-page ad in *The New York Times* underscores how organized are the forces confronting MartinJackson. The groups include online pharmacies, senior-citizen groups and patient advocates. The ad says, "MartinJackson is taking away the right of arthritis victims to affordable prescription drugs." The media frenzy has already begun. The newswires and the morning television shows are particular danger zones.

MartinJackson's first response had been a public service announcement claiming that buying drugs over the Internet is not safe. The tactic backfired. The message was scoffed at, and begged the question, "Why don't you sell the drug to us at a reasonable price in a safer venue?"

The CEO has informed the board that its decision to cut shipments is non-negotiable.

The tasks at hand:

- Decide if the company wants to proactively defend its actions, or accept a few bad press days, hoping the hubbub will subside.
- Identify a spokesperson(s) to counteract accusations from elderly

"victims" of the company's imputed callousness. Should the company rely on its own articulate C-suite spokespersons–especially the dynamic CEO–or tap outside supporters for public commentary? If so, who should those spokespersons be and what should they say?

- In general, what message points are now required? Should they address the specific situation and the business necessity of cutting Canadian shipments? Should they go beyond the specific situation and stress the social value of the company's other products and its valuable research contributions?
- How can you argue "business necessity" when your competitors are not cutting shipments to Canada?
- What lesson do you draw from the failure of the public service announcement about the safety of buying drugs on the Internet?
- What sort of specific responses to imminent events–especially protest marches and boycotts–are advisable? Is there a single message point to address all such events, or should the company be prepared to reformulate its message with each new sortie by the opposition?
- Do you pull or change your current marketing campaign for Vigorate?
- What role, if any, might an alternative advertising or public service campaign play?
- What role, if any, might a company-sponsored philanthropic initiative play?

Congress will be taking up the issue later this year, so the stakes are sky-high. Not only is your immediate competitive position in jeopardy, but a political setback on the Hill might permanently put you at the mercy of Canada-based suppliers underselling your retail prescriptions to millions of customers.

VII. A Law Firm in Trouble: Controlling the Story

1. It's Monday morning, and John Parsons, the managing partner of Burns & Beltvay, a well-known Washington, D.C., law firm, has just received word that the entire government contracts practice group will be moving to a competitor firm. There are 12 letters of resignation on his desk, five from partners and seven from associates. While the ink is still fresh on the letters, a call from an *American Lawyer* reporter lands on Parsons' voice mail.

Parsons doesn't know how many of his other partners are aware of what has happened, although relations between the executive committee and the government contracts lawyers had been conspicuously strained for months. In some ways, their departure is not altogether negative, as the most profitable practice groups by far are the fairly new corporate and biotech groups that have prospered despite the tech downturn. It's a chance to really clean shop and drive firm-wide profits higher.

The possibilities confronting the firm are thus either very positive or, if the wrong messages are sent, very negative. There are a few complications as well, including low associate satisfaction rankings and a London office (also corporate) that has been hemorrhaging money. It's a firm in transition, with strong liabilities and assets in its current position.

The *American Lawyer* interview is crucial. It will set the tone for any other interview on the subject. *AmLaw's* sister publications will likely pick up Parsons' comments as well, especially in Texas and Florida where the firm has handled high-profile matters. If the U.K. press pays attention, they'll pounce hard and focus particularly on the faltering London office (which has so far escaped under the local-media radar screen).

Challenge: Evolve the right message point. Make it sound believable. Assuage the other partners.

2. Parsons finishes the *American Lawyer* interview around 2 pm. At 3 pm, he meets Joe Farrell, head of the firm's small employment practice, in the coffee room. "Oh by the way," says Farrell, "some guy from *The Washington Post* called me about DimStar." DimStar is a major biotech company based in Maryland that the firm helped grow from a start-up. "I guess that complaint against Thompson has gotten out."

Parsons is appalled. A DimStar secretary had filed suit against DimStar and CFO Jack Thompson for sexual harassment. Farrell fears that, if the press has picked up on it, they will piggyback the story on a year-old harassment charge against a partner in the firm.

That case was settled quietly. Fortunately, it was more or less ignored at the time by the legal press. Unfortunately, it did receive a little ink and was posted on legal news Web sites. Anyone covering the DimStar situation might well stumble on it. The accused partner is still with Burns & Beltvay and has handled transactions for DimStar.

For an enterprising reporter, there's a real feature on the firm lurking in the wings. Such a feature would portray an out-of-control partnership that is harassing secretaries, losing lawyers in droves, torturing associates and wasting money on ill-advised transatlantic ventures.

Taken in pieces, each component is explainable. Taken as a whole, it's a damaging portrait—and the DimStar harassment problem is just the spark to ignite such a firm-wide fire, even though the complaint against Jack Thompson actually happened someplace else.

It is therefore imperative that Burns & Beltvay help DimStar manage the Thompson media crisis as effectively as possible, not only as a matter of client service but of direct self-interest as well. Choice of spokesperson to respond to the media on behalf of DimStar is crucial. So are the message points. So are the responses to any reporter who may ask about the year-old sex complaint against Burns & Beltvay, or even mention it casually.

Challenge: Help Farrell and DimStar manage the media in a way that minimizes the story. Prepare for the worst if the old allegation against Burns & Beltvay is revived. Fragment the Burns & Beltvay story to discourage reporters from piecing together these various discrete problems into one damning whole.

VIII. A Celebrity Client: The Guy They Love to Hate

Joe Walker—one of the most arrogant and widely disliked, but perennially high-scoring, stars in the National Basketball Association—is arrested for assault and battery. The victim is in a coma. The evidence against Walker is strong but not conclusive. Walker's lawyer has made a predictable assertion of innocence on the courtroom steps.

Reporters are clamoring to talk to Walker, and his lawyer naturally counsels his client not to give any interviews. But Walker has already told one sports reporter that his victim was "just a jerk."

Reporters are also clamoring to talk to Susan Farrell, Walker's agent.

Farrell is very worried. Walker's team is not a playoff contender, so the PR liabilities of keeping Walker on the roster could outweigh any benefits of letting him play. There is a morals clause in Walker's contract. If there is enough public outrage, the team might well exercise it. That would be bad news for Farrell; her stake is 15 percent of $20 million.

Farrell is convinced that someone besides Walker's lawyer ought to talk to the press, as daily coverage has been rehashing past misdeeds. Farrell herself is a former publicist and well liked by sports writers. She also attracts a lot of media attention on her own, having been the first woman agent to represent athletes at this level.

Farrell decides to grant an interview. After all, she might as well. With a few more days of bad press, Walker could be out of a job and Farrell out of a commission. But first she needs to get a few message points in line. She's also wondering if it might actually be beneficial to do a joint press interview with Walker, despite his lawyer's prohibition.

Suddenly her secretary rings. Two old friends from the *Post Gazette* would like to see her. She decides to see them and talk about Walker.

Her audience is the public and also the team management. Her goal is to save Walker's job, at least until the case is decided in court.

What should she say?

Appendix C

Source Contacts

Chapter 1
Value of Media Management
Lawyers
Steven B. Hantler
Assistant General Counsel for
Government and Regulation
DaimlerChrysler
sbh2@daimlerchrysler.com

Sandy S. McMath
Partner
Sandy S. McMath & Associates
sandymcmath@aol.com

William R. Sampson
Incoming President
DRI (Defense Research Institute)
Partner
Shook, Hardy & Bacon L.L.P.
wsampson@shb.com

Chapter 2
Crisis Teams
Lawyer
John M. Callagy
Chairman
Kelley Drye & Warren LLP
jcallagy@kelleydrye.com

Corporate Communications
Nancy Banks
Director, Public Relations
Michelin, North America
nancy.banks@us.michelin.com

Chris Hinze
Marketing & Communications
Director
Ernst & Young
christopher.hinze@uk.ey.com

Chapter 3
Crisis Plans
Corporate Communications
Nancy Banks
Director, Public Relations
Michelin, North America
nancy.banks@us.michelin.com

Jan Drummond
Former Senior Director, External
Communications
Sears, Roebuck and Co.

Others
David B. Armon
President
PR Newswire Association LLC
dave.armon@prnewswire.com

Justin Szlasa
President
Triplebridge Consulting Ltd.
jszlasa@triplebridge.com

Chapter 4
Print Interview
Lawyers
Christopher G. Caldwell
Partner
Caldwell, Leslie, Newcombe & Pettit
caldwell@clnp.com

William R. Sampson
Incoming President
DRI (Defense Research Institute)
Partner
Shook, Hardy & Bacon L.L.P.
wsampson@shb.com

Howard D. Scher
Partner
Buchanan Ingersoll PC
scherhd@bipc.com

Mark S. Ostrau
Partner
Fenwick & West LLP
mostrau@fenwick.com

William J. Rochelle III
Partner
Fulbright & Jaworski L.L.P.
wrochelle@fulbright.com

Chapter 9
Cross-Border
Lawyers
Martin D. Beirne
Partner
Beirne, Maynard & Parsons L.L.P
MBeirne@BMPllp.com

Ian S. Forrester
Partner
White & Case LLP
iforrester@whitecase.com

Thomas B. Wilner
Partner
Shearman & Sterling LLP
twilner@shearman.com

Chapter 10
Law Firms in Trouble
Lawyer
Leslie Corwin
Partner
Greenberg Traurig, LLP
corwinl@gtlaw.com

Chapter 11
Offense
Richard Berman
President
Berman and Company
berman@bermanco.com

Eric Dezenhall
President
Nichols Dezenhall
dezenhall@ndez.com

Appendix A
Lawyer
Michael J. Wagner
Partner
Baker & McKenzie
michael.j.wagner@bakernet.com

Also Consulted:
Diane Schwartz
Publisher
PRNews
PBI Media Inc.
dschwartz@pbimedia.com